Jesus t [illegible] 8)

And

The Wanderer

by

Kahlil Gibran

The Echo Library 2009

Published by

The Echo Library

Echo Library
131 High St.
Teddington
Middlesex TW11 8HH

www.echo-library.com

Please report serious faults in the text to complaints@echo-library.com

ISBN 978-1-40682-914-3

TABLE OF CONTENTS

JAMES THE SON OF ZEBEDEE

UPON A DAY IN THE SPRING OF THE YEAR Jesus stood in the market-place of Jerusalem and He spoke to the multitudes of the kingdom of heaven.

And He accused the scribes and the Pharisees of setting snares and digging pitfalls in the path of those who long after the kingdom; and He denounced them.

Now amongst the crowd was a company of men who defended the Pharisees and the scribes, and they sought to lay hands upon Jesus and upon us also.

But He avoided them and turned aside from them, and walked towards the north gate of the city.

And He said to us, "My hour has not yet come. Many are the things I have still to say unto you, and many are the deeds I shall yet perform ere I deliver myself up to the world."

Then He said, and there was joy and laughter in His voice, "Let us go into the North Country and meet the spring. Come with me to the hills, for winter is past and the snows of Lebanon are descending to the valleys to sing with the brooks.

"The fields and the vineyards have banished sleep and are awake to greet the sun with their green figs and tender grapes."

And He walked before us and we followed Him, that day and the next.

And upon the afternoon of the third day we reached the summit of Mount Hermon, and there He stood looking down upon the cities of the plains.

And His face shone like molten gold, and He outstretched His arms and He said to us, "Behold the earth in her green raiment, and see how the streams have hemmed the edges of her garments with silver.

"In truth the earth is fair and all that is upon her is fair.

"But there is a kingdom beyond all that you behold, and therein I shall rule. And if it is your choice, and if it is indeed your desire, you too shall come and rule with me.

"My face and your faces shall not be masked; our hand shall hold neither sword nor sceptre, and our subjects shall love us in peace and shall not be in fear of us."

Thus spoke Jesus, and unto all the kingdoms of the earth I was blinded, and unto all the cities of walls and towers; and it was in my heart to follow the Master to His kingdom.

Then just at that moment Judas of Iscariot stepped forth. And he walked close up to Jesus, and spoke and said, "Behold, the kingdoms of the world are vast, and behold the cities of David and Solomon shall prevail against the Romans. If you will be the king of the Jews we shall stand beside you with sword and shield and we shall overcome the alien."

But when Jesus heard this He turned upon Judas, and His face was filled with wrath. And He spoke in a voice terrible as the thunder of the sky and He said, "Get you behind me, Satan. Think you that I came down the years to rule an ant-hill for a day?

"My throne is a throne beyond your vision. Shall he whose wings encircle the earth seek shelter in a nest abandoned and forgotten?

"Shall the living be honored and exalted by the wearer of shrouds?

"My kingdom is not of this earth, and my seat is not builded upon the skulls of your ancestors.

"If you seek aught save the kingdom of the spirit then it were better for you to leave me here, and go down to the caves of your dead, where the crowned heads of yore hold court in their tombs and may still be bestowing honors upon the bones of your forefathers.

"Dare you tempt me with a crown of dross, when my forehead seeks the Pleiades, or else your thorns?

"Were it not for a dream dreamed by a forgotten race I would not suffer your sun to rise upon my patience, nor your moon to throw my shadow across your path.

"Were it not for a mother's desire I would have stripped me of the swaddling-clothes and escaped back to space.

"And were it not for sorrow in all of you I would not have stayed to weep.

"Who are you and what are you, Judas Iscariot? And why do you tempt me?

"Have you in truth weighed me in the scale and found me one to lead legions of pygmies, and to direct chariots of the shapeless against an enemy that encamps only in your hatred and marches nowhere but in your fear?

"Too many are the worms that crawl about my feet, and I will give them no battle. I am weary of the jest, and weary of pitying the creepers who deem me coward because I will not move among their guarded walls and towers.

"Pity it is that I must needs pity to the very end. Would that I could turn my steps towards a larger world where larger men dwell. But how shall I?

"Your priest and your emperor would have my blood. They shall be satisfied ere I go hence. I would not change the course of the law. And I would not govern folly.

"Let ignorance reproduce itself until it is weary of its own off spring. "Let the blind lead the blind to the pitfall.

"And let the dead bury the dead till the earth be choked with its own bitter fruit.

"My kingdom is not of, the earth. My kingdom shall be where two or three of you shall meet in love, and in wonder at the loveliness of life, and in good cheer, and in remembrance of me."

Then of a sudden He turned to Judas, and He said, "Get you behind me, man. Your kingdoms shall never be in my kingdom."

And now it was twilight, and He turned to us and said, "Let us go down. The night is upon us. Let us walk in light while the light is with us."

Then He went down from the hills and we followed Him. And Judas followed afar off.

And when we reached the lowland it was night.

And Thomas, the son of Diophanes, said unto Him, "Master, it is dark now, and we can no longer see the way. If it is in your will, lead us to the lights of yonder village where we may find meat and shelter."

And Jesus answered Thomas, and He said, "I have led you to the heights when you were hungry, and I have brought you down to the plains with a greater hunger. But I cannot stay with you this night. I would be alone."

Then Simon Peter stepped forth, and said: "Master, suffer us not to go alone in the dark. Grant that we may stay with you even here on this byway. The night and the shadows of the night will not linger, and the morning shall soon find us if you will but stay with us."

And Jesus answered, "This night the foxes shall have their holes, and the birds of the air their nests, but the Son of Man has not where on earth to lay His head. And indeed I would now be alone. Should you desire me you will find me again by the lake where I found you."

Then we walked away from Him with heavy hearts, for it was not in our will to leave Him.

Many times did we stop and turn our faces towards Him, and we saw Him in lonely majesty, moving westward.

The only man among us who did not turn to behold Him in His aloneness was Judas Iscariot.

And from that day Judas became sullen and distant. And me thought there was danger in the sockets of his eyes.

ANNA THE MOTHER OF MARY

JESUS THE SON OF MY DAUGHTER, WAS BORN here in Nazareth in the month of January. And the night that Jesus was born we were visited by men from the East. They were Persians who came to Esdraelon with the caravans of the Midianites on their way to Egypt. And because they did not find rooms at the inn they sought shelter in our house.

And I welcomed them and I said, "My daughter has given birth to a son this night. Surely you will forgive me if I do not serve you as it behooves a hostess."

Then they thanked me for giving them shelter. And after they had supped they said to me: "We would see the new-born."

Now the Son of Mary was beautiful to behold, and she too was comely.

And when the Persians beheld Mary and her babe, they took gold and silver from their bags, and myrrh and frankincense, and laid them all at the feet of the child.

Then they fell down and prayed in a strange tongue which we did not understand.

And when I led them to the bedchamber prepared for them they walked as if they were in awe at what they had seen.

When morning was come they left us and followed the road to Egypt.

But at parting they spoke to me and said: "The child is but a day old, yet we have seen the light of our God in His eyes and the smile of our God upon His mouth.

"We bid you protect Him that He may protect you all."

And so saying, they mounted their camels and we saw them no more.

Now Mary seemed not so much joyous in her first-born, as full of wonder and surprise.

She would look long upon her babe, and then turn her face to the window and gaze far away into the sky as if she saw visions.

And there were valleys between her heart and mine.

And the child grew in body and spirit, and He was different from other children. He was aloof and hard to govern, and I could not lay my hand upon Him.

But He was beloved by everyone in Nazareth, and in my heart I knew why.

Oftentimes He would take away our food to give to the passer-by. And He would give other children the sweetmeat I had given Him, before He had tasted it with His own mouth. He would climb the trees of my orchard to get the fruits, but never to eat them Himself.

And He would race with other boys, and sometimes, because He was swifter of foot, He would delay so that they might pass the stake ere He should reach it.

And sometimes when I led Him to His bed He would say, "Tell my mother and the others that only my body will sleep. My mind will be with them till their mind come to my morning."

And many other wondrous words He said when He was a boy, but I am too old to remember.

Now they tell me I shall see Him no more. But how shall I believe what they say?

I still hear His laughter, and the sound of His running about my house. And whenever I kiss the cheek of my daughter His fragrance returns to my heart, and His body seems to fill my arms.

But is it not passing strange that my daughter does not speak of her first-born to me?

Sometimes it seems that my longing for Him is greater than hers. She stands as firm before the day as if she were a bronzen image, while my heart melts and runs into streams.

Perhaps she knows what I do not know. Would that she might tell me also.

ASSAPH

CALLED THE ORATOR OF TYRE

WHAT SHALL I SAY OF HIS SPEECH? PERHAPS something about His person lent power to His words and swayed those who heard Him. For He was comely, and the sheen of the day was upon His countenance.

Men and women gazed at Him more than they listened to His argument. But at times He spoke with the power of a spirit, and that spirit had authority over those who heard Him.

In my youth I had heard the orators of Rome and Athens and Alexandria. The young Nazarene was unlike them all.

They assembled their words with an art to enthrall the ear, but when you heard Him your heart would leave you and go wandering into regions not yet visited.

He would tell a story or relate a parable, and the like of His stories and parables had never been heard in Syria. He seemed to spin them out of the seasons, even as time spins the years and the generations.

He would begin a story thus: "The ploughman went forth to the field to sow his seeds."

Or, "Once there was a rich man who had many vineyards." Or, "A shepherd counted his sheep at eventide and found that one sheep was missing."

And such words would carry His listeners into their simpler selves, and into the ancient of their days.

At heart we are all ploughmen, and we all love the vineyard. And in the pastures of our memory there is a shepherd and a flock and the lost sheep;

And there is the ploughshare and the winepress and the threshing-floor.

He knew the source of our older self, and the persistent thread of which we are woven.

The Greek and the Roman orators spoke to their listeners of life as it seemed to the mind. The Nazarene spoke of a longing that lodged in the heart.

They saw life with eyes only a little clearer than yours and mine. He saw life in the light of God.

I often think that He spoke to the crowd as a mountain would speak to the plain.

And in His speech there was a power that was not commanded by the orators of Athens or of Rome.

MARY MAGDALEN

IT WAS IN THE MONTH OF JUNE WHEN I SAW Him for the first time. He was walking in the wheat field when I passed by with my handmaidens, and He was alone.

The rhythm of His step was different from other men's, and the movement of His body was like naught I had seen before.

Men do not pace the earth in that manner. And even now I do not know whether He walked fast or slow.

My handmaidens pointed their fingers at Him and spoke in shy whispers to one another. And I stayed my steps for a moment, and raised my hand to hail Him. But He did not turn His face, and He did not look at me. And I hated Him. I was swept back into myself, and I was as cold as if I had been in a snow-drift. And I shivered.

That night I beheld Him in my dreaming; and they told me afterward that I screamed in my sleep and was restless upon my bed.

It was in the month of August that I saw Him again, through my window. He was sitting in the shadow of the cypress tree across my garden, and He was as still as if He had been carved out of stone, like the statues in Antioch and other cities of the North Country. And my slave, the Egyptian, came to me and said, "That man is here again. He is sitting there across your garden."

And I gazed at Him, and my soul quivered within me, for He was beautiful.

His body was single and each part seemed to love every other part.

Then I clothed myself with raiment of Damascus, and I left my house and walked towards Him.

Was it my aloneness, or was it His fragrance, that drew me to Him? Was it a hunger in my eyes that desired comeliness, or was it His beauty that sought the light of my eyes?

Even now I do not know.

I walked to Him with my scented garments and my golden sandals, the sandals the Roman captain had given me, even these sandals. And when I reached Him, I said, "Good-morrow to you."

And He said, "Good-morrow to you, Miriam."

And He looked at me, and His night-eyes saw me as no man had seen me. And suddenly I was as if naked, and I was shy.

Yet He had only said, "Good-morrow to you."

And then I said to Him, "Will you not come to my house?"

And He said, "Am I not already in your house?"

I did not know what He meant then, but I know now. And I said Will you not have wine and bread with me?"

And He said, "Yes, Miriam, but not now."

NOT NOW, NOT NOW, He said. And the voice of the sea was in those two words, and the voice of the wind and the trees. And when He said them unto me, life spoke to death.

For mind you, my friend, I was dead. I was a woman who had divorced her soul. I was living apart from this self which you now see. I belonged to all men, and to none. They called me harlot, and a woman possessed of seven devils. I was cursed, and I was envied.

But when His dawn-eyes looked into my eyes all the stars of my night faded away, and I became Miriam, only Miriam, a woman lost to the earth she had known, and finding herself in new places.

And now again I said to Him, "Come into my house and share bread and wine with me."

And He said, "Why do you bid me to be your guest?"

And I said, "I beg you to come into my house." And it was all that was sod in me, and all that was sky in me calling unto Him.

Then He looked at me, and the noontide of His eyes was upon me, and He said, "You have many lovers, and yet I alone love you. Other men love themselves in your nearness. I love you in your self. Other men see a beauty in you that shall fade away sooner than their own years. But I see in you a beauty that shall not fade away, and in the autumn of your days that beauty shall not be afraid to gaze at itself in the mirror, and it shall not be off ended.

I alone love the unseen in you."

Then He said in a low voice, "Go away now. If this cypress tree is yours and you would not have me sit in its shadow, I will walk my way."

And I cried to Him and I said, "Master, come to my house. I have incense to burn for you, and a silver basin for your feet. You are a stranger and yet not a stranger. I entreat you, come to my house."

Then He stood up and looked at me even as the seasons might look down upon the field, and He smiled. And He said again: "All men love you for themselves. I love you for yourself."

And then He walked away.

But no other man ever walked the way He walked. Was it a breath born in my garden that moved to the east? Or was it a storm that would shake all things to their foundations?

I knew not, but on that day the sunset of His eyes slew the dragon in me, and I became a woman, I became Miriam, Miriam of Mijdel.

PHILEMON A GREEK APOTHECARY

THE NAZARENE WAS THE MASTER PHYSICIAN OF His people. No other man knew so much of our bodies and of their elements and properties.

He made whole those who were afflicted with diseases unknown to the Greeks and the Egyptians. They say He even called back the dead to life. And whether this be true or not true, it declares His power; for only to him who has wrought great things is the greatest ever attributed.

They say also that Jesus visited India and the Country between the Two Rivers, and that there the priests revealed to Him the knowledge of all that is hidden in the recesses of our flesh.

Yet that knowledge may have been given Him direct by the gods, and not through the priests. For that which has remained unknown to all men for an eon may be disclosed to one man in but a moment. And Apollo may lay his hand on the heart of the obscure and make it wise.

Many doors were open to the Tyrians and the Thebans, and to this man also certain sealed doors were opened. He entered the temple of the soul, which is the body; and He beheld the evil spirits that conspire against our sinews, and also the good spirits that spin the threads thereof.

Methinks it was by the power of opposition and resistance that He healed the sick, but in a manner unknown to our philosophers. He astonished fever with His snow-like touch and it retreated; and He surprised the hardened limbs with His own calm and they yielded to Him and were at peace.

He knew the ebbing sap within the furrowed bark-but how He reached the sap with His fingers I do not know. He knew the sound steel underneath the rust-but how He freed the sword and made it shine no man can tell.

Sometimes it seems to me that He heard the murmuring pain of all things that grow in the sun, and that then He lifted them up and supported them, not only by His own knowledge, but also by disclosing to them their own power to rise and become whole.

Yet He was not much concerned with Himself as a physician. He was rather preoccupied with the religion and the politics of this land. And this I regret, for first of all things we must needs be sound of body.

But these Syrians, when they are visited by an illness, seek an argument rather than medicine.

And pity it is that the greatest of all their physicians chose rather to be but a maker of speeches in the market-place.

SIMON WHO WAS CALLED PETER

I WAS ON THE SHORE OF THE LAKE OF GALILEE WHEN I first beheld Jesus my Lord and my Master.

My brother Andrew was with me and we were casting our net into the waters.

The waves were rough and high and we caught but few fish. And our hearts were heavy.

Suddenly Jesus stood near us, as if He had taken form that very moment, for we had not seen Him approaching.

He called us by our names, and He said, "If you will follow me I will lead you to an inlet where the fishes are swarming."

And as I looked at His face the net fell from my hands, for a flame kindled within me and I recognized Him.

And my brother Andrew spoke and said, "We know all the inlets upon these shores, and we know also that on a windy day like this the fish seek a depth beyond our nets."

And Jesus answered, "Follow me to the shores of a greater sea. I shall make you fishers of men. And your net shall never be empty."

And we abandoned our boat and our net and followed Him. I myself was drawn by a power, viewless, that walked beside His person.

I walked near Him, breathless and full of wonder, and my brother Andrew was behind us, bewildered and amazed.

And as we walked on the sand I made bold and said unto Him, "Sir, I and my brother will follow your footsteps, and where you go we too will go. But if it please you to come to our house this night, we shall be graced by your visit. Our house is not large and our ceiling not high, and you will sit at but a frugal meal. Yet if you will abide in our hovel it will be to us a palace. And would you break bread with us, we in your presence were to be envied by the princes of the land."

And He said, "Yea, I will be your guest this night."

And I rejoiced in my heart. And we walked behind Him in silence until we reached our house.

And as we stood at the threshold Jesus said, Peace be to this house, and to those who dwell it."

Then He entered and we followed Him.

My wife and my wife's mother and my daughter stood before Him and they worshipped Him; then they knelt before Him and kissed the hem of His sleeve.

They were astonished that He, the chosen and the well beloved, had, come to be our guest; for they had already seen Him by the River Jordan when John the Baptist had proclaimed Him before the people.

And straightway my wife and my wife's mother began to prepare the supper.

My brother Andrew was a shy man, but his faith in Jesus was deeper than my faith.

And my daughter, who was then but twelve years old, stood by Him and held His garment as if she were in fear He would leave us and go out again into the night. She clung to Him like a lost sheep that has found its shepherd.

Then we sat at the board, and He broke the bread and poured the wine; and He turned to us saying, "My friends, grace me now in sharing this food with me, even as the Father has graced us in giving it unto us."

These words He said ere He touched a morsel, for He wished to follow an ancient custom that the honored guest becomes the host.

And as we sat with Him around the board we felt as if we were sitting at the feast of the great King.

My daughter Petronelah, who was young and unknowing, gazed at His face and followed the movements of His hands. And I saw a veil of tears in her eyes.

When He left the board we followed Him and sat about Him in the vine-arbour. And He spoke to us and we listened, and our hearts fluttered within us like birds.

He spoke of the second birth of man, and of the opening of the gates of the heavens; and of angels descending and bringing peace and good cheer to all men, and of angels ascending to the throne bearing the longings of men to the Lord God.

Then He looked into my eyes and gazed into the depths of my heart. And He said, "I have chosen you and your brother, and you must needs come with me. You have labored and you have been heavy-laden. Now I shall give you rest. Take up my yoke and learn of me, for in my heart is peace, and your soul shall find abundance and a home-coming."

When He spoke thus I and my brother stood up before Him, and I said to Him, "Master, we will follow you to the ends of the earth. And if our burden were as heavy as the mountain we would bear it with you in gladness. And should we fall by the wayside we shall know that we have fallen on the way to heaven, and we shall be satisfied."

And my brother Andrew spoke and said,

Master, we would be threads between your hands and your loom. Weave us into the cloth if you will, for we would be in the raiment of the Most High."

And my wife raised her face, and the tears were upon her cheeks and she spoke with joy, and she said, "Blessed are you who come in the name of the Lord. Blessed is the womb that carried you, and the breast that gave you milk."

And my daughter, who was but twelve years old, sat at His feet and she nestled close to Him.

And the mother of my wife, who sat at the threshold, said not a word. She only wept in silence and her shawl was wet with her tears.

Then Jesus walked over to her and He raised her face to His face and He said to her, "You are the mother of all these. You weep for joy, and I will keep your tears in my memory."

And now the old moon rose above the horizon. And Jesus gazed upon it for a moment, and then He turned to us and said, "It is late. Seek your beds, and may God visit your repose. I will be here in this arbour until dawn. I have cast my net this day and I have caught two men; I am satisfied, and now I bid you good-night."

Then my wife's mother said, "But we have laid your bed in the house, I pray you enter and rest."

And He answered her saying, "I would indeed rest, but not under a roof. Suffer me to lie this night under the canopy of the grapes and the stars."

And she made haste and brought out the mattress and the pillows and the coverings. And He smiled on her and He said, "Behold, I shall lie down upon a bed twice made."

Then we left Him and entered into the house, and my daughter was the last one to enter. And her eyes were upon Him until I had closed the door.

Thus for the first time I knew my Lord and Master.

And though it was many years ago, it still seems but of today.

CAIAPHAS

THE HIGH PRIEST

IN SPEAKING OF THAT MAN JESUS AND OF His death let us consider two salient facts: the Torah must needs be held in safety by us, and this kingdom must needs be protected by Rome.

Now that man was defiant to us and to Rome. He poisoned the mind of the simple people, and He led them as if by magic against us and against Caesar.

My own slaves, both men and women, after hearing Him speak in the market-place, turned sullen and rebellious. Some of them left my house and escaped to the desert whence they came.

Forget not that the Torah is our foundation and our tower of strength. No man shall undermine us while we have this power to restrain his hand, and no man shall overthrow Jerusalem so long as its walls stand upon the ancient stone that David laid.

If the seed of Abraham is indeed to live and thrive this soil must remain undefiled.

And that man Jesus was a defiler and a corrupter. We slew Him with a conscience both deliberate and clean. And we shall slay all those who would debase the laws of Moses or seek to befoul our sacred heritage. We and Pontius Pilatus knew the danger in that man, and that it was wise to bring Him to an end.

I shall see that His followers come to the same end, and the echo of His word to the same silence.

If Judea is to live all men who oppose her must be brought down to the dust. And ere Judea shall die I will cover my gray head with ashes even as did Samuel the prophet, and I will tear off this garment of Aaron and clothe me in sackcloth until I go hence for ever.

JOANNA

THE WIFE OF HEROD'S STEWARD

JESUS WAS NEVER MARRIED BUT HE WAS A friend of women, and He knew them as they would be known in sweet comradeship.

And He loved children as they would be loved in faith and understanding.

In the light of His eyes there was a father and a brother and a son.

He would hold a child upon His knees and say, "Of such is your might and your freedom; and of such is the kingdom of the spirit."

They say that Jesus heeded not the law of Moses, and that He was over-forgiving to the prostitutes of Jerusalem and the country side.

I myself at that time was deemed a prostitute, for I loved a man who was not my husband, and he was a Sadducee.

And on a day the Sadducees came upon me in my house when my lover was with me, and they seized me and held me, and my lover walked away and left me.

Then they led me to the market-place where Jesus was teaching.

It was their desire to hold me up before Him as a test and a trap for Him.

But Jesus judged me not. He laid shame upon those who would have had me shamed, and He reproached them.

And He bade me go my way.

And after that all the tasteless fruit of life turned sweet to my mouth, and the scentless blossoms breathed fragrance into my nostrils. I became a woman without a tainted memory, and I was free, and my head was no longer bowed down.

RAFCA THE BRIDE OF CANA

THIS HAPPENED BEFORE HE WAS KNOWN TO THE PEOPLE.

I was in my mother's garden tending the rose-bushes, when He stopped at our gate.

And He said, "I am thirsty. Will you give me water from your well?"

And I ran and brought the silver cup, and filled it with water; and I poured into it a few drops from the jasmine vial.

And He drank deep and was pleased.

Then He looked into my eyes and said, "My blessing shall be upon you."

When He said that I felt as it were a gust of wind rushing through my body. And I was no longer shy; and I said, "Sir, I am betrothed to a man of Cana in Galilee. And I shall be married on the fourth day of the coming week. Will you not come to my wedding and grace my marriage with your presence?"

And He answered, "I will come, my child."

Mind you, He said, "My child," yet He was but a youth, and I was nearly twenty.

Then He walked on down the road.

And I stood at the gate of our garden until my mother called me into the house. On the fourth day of the following week I was taken to the house of my bridegroom and given in marriage.

And Jesus came, and with Him His mother and His brother James.

And they sat around the wedding-board with our guests whilst my maiden comrades sang the wedding-songs of Solomon the King. And Jesus ate our food and drank our wine and smiled upon me and upon the others.

And He heeded all the songs of the lover bringing his beloved into his tent; and of the young vineyard-keeper who loved the daughter of the lord of the vineyard and led her to his mother's house; and of the prince who met the beggar maiden and bore her to his realm and crowned her with the crown of his fathers.

And it seemed as if He were listening to yet other songs also, which I could not hear.

At sundown the father of my bridegroom came to the mother of Jesus and whispered saying, "We have no more wine for our guests. And the day is not yet over."

And Jesus heard the whispering, and He said, "The cup bearer knows that there is still more wine."

And so it was indeed-and as long as the guests remained there was fine wine for all who would drink. Presently Jesus began to speak with us. He spoke of the wonders of earth and heaven; of sky flowers that bloom when night is upon the earth, and of earth flowers that blossom when the day hides the stars.

And He told us stories and parables, and His voice enchanted us so that we gazed upon Him as if seeing visions, and we forgot the cup and the plate.

And as I listened to Him it seemed as if I were in a land distant and unknown.

After a while one of the guests said to the father of my bridegroom, "You have kept the best wine till the end of the feast. Other hosts do not so."

And all believed that Jesus had wrought a miracle, that they should have more wine and better at the end of the wedding-feast than at the beginning.

I too thought that Jesus had poured the wine, but I was not astonished; for in His voice I had already listened to miracles.

And afterwards indeed, His voice remained close to my heart, even until I had been delivered of my first-born child.

And now even to this day in our village and in the villages near by, the word of our guest is still remembered. And they say, "The spirit of Jesus of Nazareth is the best and the oldest wine."

A PERSIAN PHILOSOPHER IN DAMASCUS

I CANNOT TELL THE FATE OF THIS MAN, NOR CAN I SAY what shall befall His disciples.

A seed hidden in the heart of an apple is an orchard invisible. Yet should that seed fall upon a rock, it will come to naught.

But this I say: The ancient God of Israel is harsh and relentless. Israel should have another God; one who is gentle and forgiving, who would look down upon them with pity; one who would descend with the rays of the sun and walk on the path of their limitations, rather than sit for ever in the judgment seat to weigh their faults and measure their wrong-doings.

Israel should bring forth a God whose heart is not a jealous heart, and whose memory of their shortcomings is brief; one who would not avenge Himself upon them even to the third and the fourth generation.

Man here in Syria is like man in all lands. He would look into the mirror of his own understanding and therein find his deity. He would fashion the gods after his own likeness, and worship that which reflects his own image.

In truth man prays to his deeper longing, that it may rise and fulfil the sum of his desires. There is no depth beyond the soul of man, and the soul is the deep that calls unto itself; for there is no other voice to speak and there are no other ears to hear.

Even we in Persia would see our faces in the disc of the sun and our bodies dancing in the fire that we kindle upon the altars.

Now the God of Jesus, whom He called Father, would not be a stranger unto the people of Jesus, and He would fulfil their desires.

The gods of Egypt have cast off their burden of stones and fled to the Nubian desert, to be free among those who are still free from knowing.

The gods of Greece and Rome are vanishing into their own sunset. They were too much like men to live in the ecstasy of men. The groves in which their magic was born have been cut down by the axes of the Athenians and the Alexandrians.

And in this land also the high places are made low by the lawyers of Beirut and the young hermits of Antioch.

Only the old women and the weary men seek the temples of their forefathers; only the exhausted at the end of the road seek its beginning.

But this man Jesus, this Nazarene, He has spoken of a God too vast to be unlike the soul of any man, too knowing to punish, too loving to remember the sins of His creatures. And this God of the Nazarene shall pass over the threshold of the children of the earth, and He shall sit at their hearth, and He shall be a blessing within their walls and a light upon their path.

But my God is the God of Zoroaster, the God who is the sun in the sky and fire upon the earth and light in the bosom of man. And I am content. I need no other God.

DAVID ONE OF HIS FOLLOWERS

I DID NOT KNOW THE MEANING OF HIS DISCOURSES OR HIS parables until He was no longer among us. Nay, I did not understand until His words took living forms before my eyes and fashioned themselves into bodies that walk in the procession of my own day.

Let me tell you this: On a night as I sat in my house pondering, and remembering His words and His deeds that I might inscribe them in a book, three thieves entered my house. And though I knew they came to rob me of my goods, I was too mindful of what I was doing to meet them with the sword, or even to say, "What do you here?"

But I continued writing my remembrances of the Master.

And when the thieves had gone then I remembered His saying, "He who would take your cloak, let him take your other cloak also."

And I understood.

As I sat recording His words no man could have stopped me even were he to have carried away all my possessions.

For though I would guard my possessions and also my person, I know where lies the greater treasure.

LUKE

JESUS DESPISED AND SCORNED THE HYPOCRITES, and His wrath was like a tempest that scourged them. His voice was thunder in their ears and He cowed them.

In their fear of Him they sought His death; and like moles in the dark earth they worked to undermine His footsteps. But He fell not into their snares.

He laughed at them, for well He knew that the spirit shall not be mocked, nor shall it be taken in the pitfall.

He held a mirror in His hand and therein He saw the sluggard and the limping and those who stagger and fall by the roadside on the way to the summit.

And He pitied them all. He would even have raised them to His stature and He would have carried their burden. Nay, He would have bid their weakness lean on His strength.

He did not utterly condemn the liar or the thief or the murderer, but He did utterly condemn the hypocrite whose face is masked and whose hand is gloved.

Often have I pondered on the heart that shelters all who come from the wasteland to its sanctuary, yet against the hypocrite is closed and sealed.

On a day as we rested with Him in the Garden of Pomegranates, I said to Him, "Master, you forgive and console the sinner and all the weak and the infirm save only the hypocrite alone."

And He said, "You have chosen your words well when you called sinners weak and infirm. I do forgive them their weakness of body and their infirmity of spirit. For their failings have been laid upon them by their forefathers, or by the greed of their neighbours.

"But I tolerate not the hypocrite, because he himself lays a yoke upon the guileless and the yielding.

"Weaklings, whom you call sinners, are like the featherless young that fall from the nest. The hypocrite is the vulture waiting upon a rock for the death of the prey.

"Weaklings are men lost in a desert. But the hypocrite is not lost. He knows the way yet he laughs between the sand and the wind.

"For this cause I do not receive him."

Thus our Master spoke, and I did not understand. But I understand now.

Then the hypocrites of the land laid hands upon Him and they judged Him; and in so doing they deemed themselves justified. For they cited the law of Moses in the Sanhedrim in witness and evidence against Him.

And they who break the law at the rise of every dawn and break it again at sunset, brought about His death.

MATTHEW THE SERMON ON THE MOUNT

ONE HARVEST DAY JESUS CALLED US AND His other friends to the hills. The earth was fragrant, and like the daughter of a king at her wedding-feast, she wore all her jewels. And the sky was her bridegroom.

When we reached the heights Jesus stood still in the grove of laurels, and He said, "Rest here, quiet your mind and tune your heart, for I have much to tell you."

Then we reclined on the grass, and the summer flowers were all about us, and Jesus sat in our midst.

And Jesus said:

Blessed are the serene in spirit.

Blessed are they who are not held by possessions, for they shall be free.

"Blessed are they who remember their pain, and in their pain await their joy.

"Blessed are they who hunger after truth and beauty, for their hunger shall bring bread, and their thirst cool water.

Blessed are the kindly, for they shall be consoled by their own kindliness.

"Blessed are the pure in heart, for they shall be one with God. "Blessed are the merciful, for mercy shall be in their portion.

"Blessed are the peacemakers, for their spirit shall dwell above the battle, and they shall turn the potter's field into a garden.

"Blessed are they who are hunted, for they shall be swift of foot and they shall be winged.

"Rejoice and be joyful, for you have found the kingdom of heaven within you. The singers of old were persecuted when they sang of that kingdom. You too shall be persecuted, and therein lies your honor, and therein your reward.

"You are the salt of the earth; should the salt lose its savour wherewith shall the food of man's heart be salted?

"You are the light of the world. Put not that light under a bushel. Let it shine rather from the summit, to those who seek the City of God.

"Think not I came to destroy the laws of the scribes and the Pharisees; for my days among you are numbered and my words are counted, and I have but hours in which to fulfil another law and reveal a new covenant.

"You have been told that you shall not kill, but I say unto you, you shall not be angry without a cause.

"You have been charged by the ancients to bring your calf and your lamb and your dove to the temple, and to slay them upon the altar, that the nostrils of God may feed upon the odour of their fat, and that you may be forgiven your failings.

"But I say unto you, would you give God that which was His own from the beginning; and would you appease Him whose throne is above the silent deep and whose arms encircle space?

"Rather, seek out your brother and be reconciled unto him ere you seek the temple; and be a loving giver unto your neighbour. For in the soul of these God has builded a temple that shall not be destroyed, and in their heart He has raised an altar that shall never perish.

"You have been told, an eye for an eye and a tooth for a tooth. But I say unto you: Resist not evil, for resistance is food unto evil and makes it strong. And only the weak would revenge themselves. The strong of soul forgive, and it is honor in the injured to forgive.

"Only the fruitful tree is shaken or stoned for food.

"Be not heedful of the morrow, but rather gaze upon today, for sufficient for today is the miracle thereof.

"Be not over-mindful of yourself when you give but be mindful of the necessity. For every giver himself receives from the Father, and that much more abundantly.

And give to each according to his need; for the Father gives not salt to the thirsty, nor a stone to the hungry, nor milk to the weaned.

"And give not that which is holy to dogs; nor cast your pearls before swine. For with such gifts you mock them; and they also shall mock your gift, and in their hate would fain destroy you.

"Lay not up for yourselves treasures that corrupt or that thieves may steal away. Lay up rather treasure which shall not corrupt nor be stolen, and whose loveliness increases when many eyes behold it. For where your treasure is, your heart is also.

"You have been told that the murderer shall be put to the sword, that the thief shall be crucified, and the harlot stoned. But I say unto you that you are not free from the wrongdoing of the murderer and the thief and the harlot, and when they are punished in the body your own spirit is darkened.

"Verily no crime is committed by one man or one woman. All crimes are committed by all. And he who pays the penalty may be breaking a link in the chain that hangs upon your own ankles. Perhaps he is paying with his sorrow the price for your passing joy.

Thus spake Jesus, and it was in my desire to kneel down and worship Him, yet in my shyness I could not move nor speak a word.

But at last I spoke; and I said, "I would pray this moment, yet my tongue is heavy. Teach me to pray." And Jesus said, "When you would pray, let your longing pronounce the words. It is in my longing now to pray thus:

"Our Father in earth and heaven, sacred is Thy name. Thy will be done with us, even as in space. Give us of Thy bread sufficient for the day. In Thy compassion forgive us and enlarge us to forgive one another. Guide us towards Thee and stretch down Thy hand to us in darkness. For Thine is the kingdom, and in Thee is our power and our fulfilment."

And it was now evening, and Jesus walked down from the hills, and all of us followed Him. And as I followed I was repeating His prayer, and remembering all that He had said; for I knew that the words that had fallen like flakes that day must set and grow firm like crystals, and that the wings that had fluttered above our heads were to beat the earth like iron hoofs.

JOHN THE SON OF ZEBEDEE

YOU HAVE REMARKED THAT SOME OF US CALL Jesus THE CHRIST, and some THE WORD, and others call Him the NAZARENE, and still others the SON OF MAN.

I will try to make these names clear in the light that is given me.

The Christ, He who was in the ancient of days, is the flame of God that dwells in the spirit of man. He is the breath of life that visits us, and takes unto Himself a body like our bodies.

He is the will of the Lord.

He is the first Word, which would speak with our voice and live in our ear that we may heed and understand.

And the Word of the Lord our God builded a house of flesh and bones, and was man like unto you and myself.

For we could not hear the song of the bodiless wind nor see our greater self walking in the mist.

Many times the Christ has come to the world, and He has walked many lands. And always He has been deemed a stranger and a madman.

Yet the sound of His voice descended never to emptiness, for the memory of man keeps that which his mind takes no care to keep. This is the Christ, the innermost and the height, who walks with man towards eternity.

Have you not heard of Him at the cross-roads of India? And in the land of the Magi, and upon the sands of Egypt?

And here in your North Country your bards of old sang of Prometheus, the fire-bringer, he who was the desire of man fulfilled, the caged hope made free; and of Orpheus, who came with a voice and a lyre to quicken the spirit in beast and man.

And know you not of Mithra the king, and of Zoroaster the prophet of the Persians, who woke from man's ancient sleep and stood at the bed of our dreaming?

We ourselves become man anointed when we meet in the Temple Invisible, once every thousand years. Then comes one forth embodied, and at His coming our silence turns to singing.

Yet our ears turn not always to listening nor our eyes to seeing.

Jesus the Nazarene was born and reared like ourselves; His mother and father were like our parents, and He was a man.

But the Christ, the Word, who was in the beginning, the Spirit who would have us live our fuller life, came unto Jesus and was with Him.

And the Spirit was the versed hand of the Lord, and Jesus was the harp. The Spirit was the psalm, and Jesus was the tune thereof.

And Jesus, the Man of Nazareth, was the host and the mouthpiece of the Christ, who walked with us in the sun and who called us His friends.

In those days the hills of Galilee and her valleys heard naught but His voice. And I was a youth then, and trod in His path and pursued His footprints.

I pursued His footprints and trod in His path, to hear the words of the Christ from the lips of Jesus of Galilee.

Now you would know why some of us call Him the Son of Man.

He Himself desired to be called by that name, for He knew the hunger and the thirst of man, and He beheld man seeking after His greater self.

The Son of Man was Christ the Gracious, who would be with us all.

He was Jesus the Nazarene who would lead all His brothers to the Anointed One, even to the Word which was in the beginning with God.

In my heart dwells Jesus of Galilee, the Man above men, the Poet who makes poets of us all, the Spirit who knocks at our door that we may wake and rise and walk out to meet truth naked and unencumbered.

A YOUNG PRIEST IN CAPERNAUM

HE WAS A MAGICIAN, WARP AND WOOF, AND a sorcerer, a man who bewildered the simple by charms and incantations. And He juggled with the words of our prophets and with the sanctities of our forefathers.

Aye, He even bade the dead be His witnesses, and the voiceless graves His forerunners and authority.

He sought the women of Jerusalem and the women of the countryside with the cunning of, the spider that seeks the fly; and they were caught in His web.

For women are weak and empty-headed, and they follow the man who would comfort their unspent passion with soft and tender words. Were it not for these women, infirm and possessed by His evil spirit, His name would have been erased from the memory of man.

And who were the men who followed Him?

They were of the horde that are yoked and trodden down. In their ignorance and fear they would never have rebelled against their rightful masters. But when He promised them high stations in His kingdom of mirage, they yielded to His fantasy as clay yields to the potter.

Know you not, the slave in his dreaming would always be master; and the weakling would be a lion?

The Galilean was a conjuror and a deceiver, a man who forgave the sins of all the sinners that He might hear HAIL and HOSANNA from their unclean mouths; and who fed the faint heart of the hopeless and the wretched that He might have ears for His voice and a retinue at His command.

He broke the sabbath with those who break that He might gain the support of the lawless; and He spoke ill of our high priests that He might win attention in the Sanhedrim, and by opposition increase His fame.

I have said often that I hated that man. Ay, I hate Him more than I hate the Romans who govern our country. Even His coming was from Nazareth, a town cursed by our prophets, a dunghill of the Gentiles, from which no good shall ever proceed.

A RICH LEVI

IN THE NEIGHBOURHOOD OF NAZARETH

HE WAS A GOOD CARPENTER. THE DOORS HE fashioned were never unlocked by thieves, and the windows he made were always ready to open to the east wind and to the west.

And He made chests of cedar wood, polished and enduring, and ploughs and pitchforks strong and yielding to the hand.

And He carved lecterns for our synagogues. He carved them out of the golden mulberry; and on both sides of the support, where the sacred book lies, He chiselled wings outspreading; and under the support, heads of bulls and doves, and large-eyed deer.

All this He wrought in the manner of the Chaldeans and the Greeks. But there was that in His skill which was neither Chaldean nor Greek.

Now this my house was builded by many hands thirty years ago. I sought builders and carpenters in all the towns of Galilee. They had each the skill and the art of building, and I was pleased and satisfied with all that they did.

But come now, and behold two doors and a window that were fashioned by Jesus of Nazareth. They in their stability mock at all else in my house.

See you not that these two doors are different from all other doors? And this window opening to the east, is it not different from other windows?

All my doors and windows are yielding to the years save these which He made. They alone stand strong against the elements.

And see those cross-beams, how he placed them; and these nails, how they are driven from one side of the board, and then caught and fastened so firmly upon the other side.

And what is passing strange is that that labourer who was worthy the wages of two men received but the wage of one man; and that same labourer now is deemed a prophet in Israel.

Had I known then that this youth with saw and plane was a prophet, I would have begged Him to speak rather than work, and then I would have overpaid Him for his words.

And now I still have many men working in my house and fields. How shall I know the man whose own hand is upon his tool, from the man upon whose hand God lays His hand?

Yea, how shall I know God's hand?

A SHEPHERD IN SOUTH LEBANON

IT WAS LATE SUMMER WHEN HE AND THREE other men first walked upon that road yonder. It was evening, and He stopped and stood there at the end of the pasture.

I was playing upon my flute, and my flock was grazing all around me. When He stopped I rose and walked over and stood before Him.

And He asked me, "Where is the grave of Elijah? Is it not somewhere near this place?"

And I answered Him, "It is there, Sir, underneath that great heap of stones. Even unto this day every passer-by brings a stone and places it upon the heap."

And He thanked me and walked away, and His friends walked behind Him.

And after three days Gamaliel who was also a shepherd, said to me that the man who had passed by was a prophet in Judea; but I did not believe him. Yet I thought of that man for many a moon.

When spring came Jesus passed once more by this pasture, and this time He was alone.

I was not playing on my flute that day for I had lost a sheep and I was bereaved, and my heart was downcast within me.

And I walked towards Him and stood still before Him, for I desired to be comforted. And He looked at me and said, "You do not play upon your flute this day. Whence is the sorrow in your eyes?"

And I answered, "A sheep from among my sheep is lost. I have sought her everywhere but I find her not. And I know not what to do."

And He was silent for a moment. Then He smiled upon me and said, "Wait here awhile and I will find your sheep." And He walked away and disappeared among the hills.

After an hour He returned, and my sheep was close beside Him. And as He stood before me, the sheep looked up into His face even as I was looking. Then I embraced her in gladness.

And He put His hand upon my shoulder and said, "From this day you shall love this sheep more than any other in your flock, for she was lost and now she is found."

And again I embraced my sheep in gladness, and she came close to me, and I was silent.

But when I raised my head to thank Jesus, He was already walking afar off, and I had not the courage to follow Him.

JOHN THE BAPTIST TO ONE OF HIS DISCIPLES

I AM NOT SILENT IN THIS FOUL HOLE WHILE THE VOICE OF Jesus is heard on the battlefield. I am not to be held nor confined while He is free.

They tell me the vipers are coiling round His loins, but I answer: The vipers shall awaken His strength, and He shall crush them with His heel.

I am only the thunder of His lightning. Though I spoke first, His was the word and the purpose.

They caught me unwarned. Perhaps they will lay hands on Him also. Yet not before He has pronounced His word in full. And He shall overcome them.

His chariot shall pass over them, and the hoofs of His horses shall trample them, and He shall be triumphant.

They shall go forth with lance and sword, but He shall meet them with the power of the Spirit.

His blood shall run upon the earth, but they themselves shall know the wounds and the pain thereof, and they shall be baptized in their tears until they are cleansed of their sins.

Their legions shall march towards His cities with rams of iron, but on their way they shall be drowned in the River Jordan.

And His walls and His towers shall rise higher, and the shields of His warriors shall shine brighter in the sun.

They say I am in league with Him, and that our design is to urge the people to rise and revolt against the kingdom of Judea.

I answer, and would that I had flames for words: if they deem this pit of iniquity a kingdom, let it then fall into destruction and be no more. Let it go the way of Sodom and Gomorrah, and let this race be forgotten by God, and this land be turned to ashes.

Aye, behind these prison walls I am indeed an ally to Jesus of Nazareth, and He shall lead my armies, horse and foot. And I myself, though a captain, am not worthy to loose the strings of His sandals.

Go to Him and repeat my words, and then in my name beg Him for comfort and blessing.

I shall not be here long. At night 'twixt waking and waking I feel slow feet with measured steps treading above this body. And when I hearken, I hear the rain falling upon my grave.

Go to Jesus, and say that John of Kedron whose soul is filled with shadows and then emptied again, prays for Him, while the grave-digger stands close by, and the swordsman outstretches his hand for his wages.

JOSEPH OF ARIMATHEA

YOU WOULD KNOW THE PRIMAL AIM OF JESUS, and I would fain tell you. But none can touch with fingers the life of the blessed vine, nor see the sap that feeds the branches.

And though I have eaten of the grapes and have tasted the new vintage at the winepress, I cannot tell you all.

I can only relate what I know of Him.

Our Master and our Beloved lived but three prophet's seasons. They were the spring of His song, the summer of His ecstasy, and the autumn of His passion; and each season was a thousand years.

The spring of His song was spent in Galilee. It was there that He gathered His lovers about Him, and it was on the shores of the blue lake that He first spoke of the Father, and of our release and our freedom.

By the Lake of Galilee we lost ourselves to find our way to the Father; and oh, the little, little loss that turned to such gain.

It was there the angels sang in our ears and bade us leave the and land for the garden of heart's desire.

He spoke of fields and green pastures; of the slopes of Lebanon where the white lilies are heedless of the caravans passing in the dust of the valley. He spoke of the wild brier that smiles in the sun and yields its incense to the passing breeze.

And He would say, "The lilies and the brier live but a day, yet that day is eternity spent in freedom."

And one evening as we sat beside the stream He said, "Behold the brook and listen to its music. Forever shall it seek the sea, and though it is for ever seeking, it sings its mystery from noon to noon.

"Would that you seek the Father as the brook seeks the sea."

Then came the summer of His ecstasy, and the June of His love was upon us. He spoke of naught then but the other man-the neighbour, the roadfellow, the stranger, and our childhood's playmates.

He spoke of the traveller journeying from the east to Egypt, of the ploughman coming home with his oxen at eventide, of the chance guest led by dusk to our door.

And He would say, "Your neighbour is your unknown self made visible. His face shall be reflected in your still waters, and if you gaze therein you shall behold your own countenance.

"Should you listen in the night, you shall hear him speak, and his words shall be the throbbing of your own heart.

"Be unto him that which you would have him be unto you.

"This is my law, and I shall say it unto you, and unto your children, and they unto their children until time is spent and generations are no more."

And on another day He said, "You shall not be yourself alone. You are in the deeds of other men, and they though unknowing are with you all your days.

"They shall not commit a crime and your hand not be with their hand.

"They shall not fall down but that you shall also fall down; and they shall not rise but that you shall rise with them.

"Their road to the sanctuary is your road, and when they seek the wasteland you too seek with them.

"You and your neighbour are two seeds sown in the field. Together you grow and together you shall sway in the wind. And neither of you shall claim the field. For a seed on its way to growth claims not even its own ecstasy.

"Today I am with you. Tomorrow I go westward; but ere I go, I say unto you that your neighbour is your unknown self made visible. Seek him in love that you may know yourself, for only in that knowledge shall you become my brothers."

Then came the autumn of His passion.

And He spoke to us of freedom, even as He had spoken in Galilee in the spring of His song; but now His words sought our deeper understanding.

He spoke of leaves that sing only when blown upon the wind; and of man as a cup filled by the ministering angel of the day to quench the thirst of another angel. Yet whether that cup is full or empty it shall stand crystalline upon the board of the Most High.

He said, "You are the cup and you are the wine. Drink of yourselves to the dregs; or else remember me and you shall be quenched."

And on our way to the southward He said,

Jerusalem, which stands in pride upon the height, shall descend to the depth of Jahannum the dark valley, and in the midst of her desolation I shall stand alone.

"The temple shall fall to dust, and around the portico you shall hear the cry of widows and orphans; and men in their haste to escape shall not know the faces of their brothers, for fear shall be upon them all.

"But even there, if two of you shall meet and utter my name and look to the west, you shall see me, and these my words shall again visit your ears."

And when we reached the hill of Bethany, He said, "Let us go to Jerusalem. The city awaits us. I will enter the gate riding upon a colt, and I will speak to the multitude.

"Many are there who would chain me, and many who would put out my flame, but in my death you shall find life and you shall be free.

"They shall seek the breath that hovers betwixt heart and mind as the swallow hovers between the field and his nest. But my breath has already escaped them, and they shall not overcome me.

"The walls that my Father has built around me shall not fall down, and the acre He has made holy shall not be profaned.

"When the dawn shall come, the sun will crown my head and I shall be with you to face the day. And that day shall be long, and the world shall not see its eventide.

"The scribes and the Pharisees say the earth is thirsty for my blood. I would quench the thirst of the earth with my blood. But the drops shall rise oak trees and maple, and the east wind shall carry the acorns to other lands."

And then He said, "Judea would have a king, and she would march against the legions of Rome.

"I shall not be her king. The diadems of Zion were fashioned for lesser brows. And the ring of Solomon is small for this finger.

"Behold my hand. See you not that it is overstrong to hold a sceptre, and over-sinewed to wield a common sword?

"Nay, I shall not command Syrian flesh against Roman. But you with my words shall wake that city, and my spirit shall speak to her second dawn. "My words shall be an invisible army with horses and chariots, and without ax or spear I shall conquer the priests of Jerusalem, and the Caesars.

"I shall not sit upon a throne where slaves have sat and ruled other slaves. Nor will I rebel against the sons of Italy.

"But I shall be a tempest in their sky, and a song in their soul.

"And I shall be remembered.

"They shall call me Jesus the Anointed."

These things He said outside the walls of Jerusalem before He entered the city.

And His words are graven as with chisels.

NATHANIEL

THEY SAY THAT JESUS OF NAZARETH WAS HUMBLE and meek.

They say that though He was a just man and righteous, He was a weakling, and was of ten confounded by the strong and the powerful; and that when He stood before men of authority He was but a lamb among lions.

But I say that Jesus had authority over men, and that He knew His power and proclaimed it among the hills of Galilee, and in the cities of Judea and Phoenicia.

What man yielding and soft would say, "I am life, and I am the way to truth"?

What man meek and lowly would say, "I am in God, our Father; and our God, the Father, is in me"?

What man unmindful of His own strength would say, "He who believes not in me believes not in this life nor in the life everlasting"?

What man uncertain of tomorrow would proclaim, "Your world shall pass away and be naught but scattered ashes ere my words shall pass away"?

Was He doubtful of Himself when He said to those who would confound Him with a harlot, He who is without sin, let him cast a stone"?

Did He fear authority when He drove the money-changers from the court of the temple, though they were licensed by the priests?

Were His wings shorn when He cried aloud, My kingdom is above your earthly kingdoms"?

Was He seeking shelter in words when He repeated again and yet again, "Destroy this temple and I will rebuild it in three days"?

Was it a coward who shook His hand in the face of the authorities and pronounced them "liars, low, filthy, and degenerate"?

Shall a man bold enough to say these things to those who ruled Judea be deemed meek and humble?

Nay. The eagle builds not his nest in the weeping willow. And the lion seeks not his den among the ferns.

I am sickened and the bowels within me stir and rise when I hear the faint-hearted call Jesus humble and meek, that they may justify their own faintheartedness; and when the downtrodden, for comfort and companionship, speak of Jesus as a worm shining by their side.

Yea, my heart is sickened by such men. It is the mighty hunter I would preach, and the mountainous spirit unconquerable.

SABA OF ANTIOCH

THIS DAY I HEARD SAUL OF TARSUS PREACHING the Christ unto the Jews of this city.

He calls himself Paul now, the apostle to the Gentiles.

I knew him in my youth, and in those days he persecuted the friends of the Nazarene. Well do I remember his satisfaction when his fellows stoned the radiant youth called Stephen.

This Paul is indeed a strange man. His soul is not the soul of a free man.

At times he seems like an animal in the forest, hunted and wounded, seeking a cave wherein he would hide his pain from the world.

He speaks not of Jesus, nor does he repeat His words. He preaches the Messiah whom the prophets of old had foretold.

And though he himself is a learned Jew he addresses his fellow Jews in Greek; and his Greek is halting, and he ill chooses his words.

But he is a man of hidden powers and his presence is affirmed by those who gather round him. And at times he assures them of what he himself is not assured.

We who knew Jesus and heard His discourses say that He taught man how to break the chains of his bondage that he might be free from his yesterdays.

But Paul is forging chains for the man of tomorrow. He would strike with his own hammer upon the anvil in the name of one whom he does not know.

The Nazarene would have us live the hour in passion and ecstasy.

The man of Tarsus would have us be mindful of laws recorded in the ancient books.

Jesus gave His breath to the breathless dead. And in my lone nights I believe and I understand.

When He sat at the board, He told stories that gave happiness to the feasters, and spiced with His joy the meat and the wine.

But Paul would prescribe our loaf and our cup.

Suffer me now to turn my eyes the other way.

SALOME TO A WOMAN FRIEND

HE WAS LIKE POPLARS SHIMMERING IN THE SUN;
And like a lake among the lonely hills,
Shining in the sun;
And like snow upon the mountain heights,
White, white in the sun.

Yea, He was like unto all these,
And I loved Him.
Yet I feared His presence.
And my feet would not carry my burden of love
That I might girdle His feet with my arms.

I would have said to Him,
"I have slain your friend in an hour of passion.
Will you forgive me my sin?
And will you not in mercy release my youth
From its blind deed,
That it may walk in your light?

I know He would have forgiven my dancing
For the saintly head of His friend.
I know He would have seen in me
An object of His own teaching.
For there was no valley of hunger He could not bridge,
And no desert of thirst He could not cross.
Yea, He was even as the poplars,
And as the lakes among the hills,
And like the snow upon Lebanon.
And I would have cooled my lips in the folds of His garment.

But He was far from me,
And I was ashamed.
And my mother held me back
When the desire to seek Him was upon me.

Whenever He passed by, my heart ached for his loveliness,
But my mother frowned at Him in contempt,
And would hasten me from the window
To my bedchamber.
And she would cry aloud saying,
Who is He but another locust-eater from the desert?

What is He but a scoffer and a renegade,
A seditious riot-monger, who would rob us of sceptre and crown,
And bid the foxes and the jackals of His accursed land
Howl in our halls and sit upon our throne?
Go hide your face from this day,
And await the day when His head shall fall down,
But not upon your platter."
These things my mother said.
But my heart would not keep her words.
I loved Him in secret,
And my sleep was girdled with flames.

He is gone now.
And something that was in me is gone also.
Perhaps it was my youth
That would not tarry here,
Since the God of youth was slain.

RACHAEL

A WOMAN DISCIPLE

I OFTEN WONDER WHETHER JESUS WAS A MAN of flesh and blood like ourselves, or a thought without a body, in the mind, or an idea that visits the vision of man.

Often it seems to me that He was but a dream dreamed by countless men and women at the same time in a sleep deeper than sleep and a dawn more serene than all dawns.

And it seems that in relating the dream, the one to the other, we began to deem it a reality that had indeed come to pass; and in giving it body of our fancy and a voice of our longing we made it a substance of our own substance.

But in truth He was not a dream. We knew Him for three years and beheld Him with our open eyes in the high tide of noon.

We touched His hands, and we followed Him from one place to another. We heard His discourses and witnessed His deeds. Think you that we were a thought seeking after more thought, or a dream in the region of dreams?

Great events always seem alien to our daily lives, though their nature may be rooted in our nature. But though they appear sudden in their coming and sudden in their passing, their true span is for years and for generations.

Jesus of Nazareth was Himself the Great Event. That man whose father and mother and brothers we know, was Himself a miracle wrought in Judea. Yea, all His own miracles, if placed at His feet, would not rise to the height of His ankles.

And all the rivers of all the years shall not carry away our remembrance of Him.

He was a mountain burning in the night, yet He was a soft glow beyond the hills. He was a tempest in the sky, yet He was a murmur in the mist of daybreak.

He was a torrent pouring from the heights to the plains to destroy all things in its path. And He was like the laughter of children.

Every year I had waited for spring to visit this valley. I had waited for the lilies and the cyclamen, and then every year my soul had been saddened within me; for ever I longed to rejoice with the spring, yet I could not.

But when Jesus came to my seasons He was indeed a spring, and in Him was the promise of all the years to come. He filled my heart with joy; and like the violets I grew, a shy thing, in the light of His coming.

And now the changing seasons of worlds not yet ours shall not erase His loveliness from this our world.

Nay, Jesus was not a phantom, nor a conception of the poets. He was man like yourself and myself. But only to sight and touch and hearing; in all other ways He was unlike us.

He was a man of joy; and it was upon the path of joy that He met the sorrows of all men. And it was from the high roofs of His sorrows that He beheld the joy of all men.

He saw visions that we did not see, and heard voices that we did not hear; and He spoke as if to invisible multitudes, and ofttimes He spoke through us to races yet unborn.

And Jesus was often alone. He was among us yet not one with us. He was upon the earth, yet He was of the sky. And only in our aloneness may we visit the land of His aloneness.

He loved us with tender love. His heart was a winepress. You and I could approach with a cup and drink therefrom.

One thing I did not use to understand in Jesus: He would make merry with His listeners; He would tell jests and play upon words, and laugh with all the fullness of His heart, even when there were distances in His eyes and sadness in His voice. But I understand now.

I often think of the earth as a woman heavy with her first child. When Jesus was born, He was the first child. And when He died, He was the first man to die.

For did it not appear to you that the earth was stilled on that dark Friday, and the heavens were at war with the heavens?

And felt you not when His face disappeared from our sight as if we were naught but memories in the mist?

CLEOPAS

OF BETHROUNE

WHEN JESUS SPOKE THE WHOLE WORLD was hushed to listen. His words were not for our ears but rather for the elements of which God made this earth.

He spoke to the sea, our vast mother, that gave us birth. He spoke to the mountain, our elder brother whose summit is a promise.

And He spoke to the angels beyond the sea and the mountain to whom we entrusted our dreams ere the clay in us was made hard in the sun.

And still His speech slumbers within our breast like a love-song half forgotten, and sometimes it burns itself through to our memory.

His speech was simple and joyous, and the sound of His voice was like cool water in a land of drought.

Once He raised His hand against the sky, and His fingers were like the branches of a sycamore tree; and He said with a great voice:

"The prophets of old have spoken to you, and your ears are filled with their speech. But I say unto you, empty your ears of what you have heard."

And these words of Jesus, "BUT I SAY UNTO YOU," were not uttered by a man of our race nor of our world; but rather by a host of seraphim marching across the sky of Judea. Again and yet again He would quote the law and the prophets, and then He would say, "BUT I SAY UNTO YOU."

Oh, what burning words, what waves of seas unknown to the shores of our mind, "BUT I SAY UNTO YOU."

What stars seeking the darkness of the soul, and what sleepless souls awaiting the dawn.

To tell of the speech of Jesus one must needs have His speech or the echo thereof.

I have neither the speech nor the echo.

I beg you to forgive me for beginning a story that I cannot end. But the end is not yet upon my lips. It is still a love song in the wind.

NAAMAN OF THE GADARENES

A FRIEND OF STEPHEN

HIS DISCIPLES ARE DISPERSED. HE GAVE THEM the legacy of pain ere He Himself was put to death. They are hunted like the deer, and the foxes of the fields, and the quiver of the hunter is yet full of arrows.

But when they are caught and led to death, they are joyous, and their faces shine like the face of the bridegroom at the wedding-feast. For He gave them also the legacy of joy.

I had a friend from the North Country, and his name was Stephen; and because he proclaimed Jesus as the Son of God, he was led to the marketplace and stoned.

And when Stephen fell to earth he outstretched his arms as if he would die as his Master had died. His arms were spread like wings ready for flight. And when the last gleam of light was fading in his eyes, with my own eyes I saw a smile upon his lips. It was a smile like the breath that comes before the end of winter for a pledge and a promise of spring.

How shall I describe it?

It seemed that Stephen was saying, "If I should go to another world, and other men should lead me to another market-place to stone me, even then I would proclaim Him for the truth which was in Him, and for that same truth which is in me now."

And I noticed that there was a man standing near, and looking with pleasure upon the stoning of Stephen.

His name was Saul of Tarsus, and it was he who had yielded Stephen to the priests and the Romans and the crowd, for stoning.

Saul was bald of head and short of stature. His shoulders were crooked and his features ill-sorted; and I liked him not.

I have been told that he is now preaching Jesus from the house tops. It is hard to believe.

But the grave halts not Jesus' walking to the enemies' camp to tame and take captive those who had opposed Him.

Still I do not like that man of Tarsus, though I have been told that after Stephen's death he was tamed and conquered on the road to Damascus. But his head is too large for his heart to be that of a true disciple.

And yet perhaps I am mistaken. I am often mistaken.

THOMAS

MY GRANDFATHER WHO WAS A LAWYER once said, "Let us observe truth, but only when truth is made manifest unto us."

When Jesus called me I heeded Him, for His command was more potent than my will; yet I kept my counsel.

When He spoke and the others were swayed like branches in the wind, I listened immovable. Yet I loved Him.

Three years ago He left us, a scattered company to sing His name, and to be His witnesses unto the nations.

At that time I was called Thomas the Doubter. The shadow of my grandfather was still upon me, and always I would have truth made manifest.

I would even put my hand in my own wound to feel the blood ere I would believe in my pain.

Now a man who loves with his heart yet holds a doubt in his mind, is but a slave in a galley who sleeps at his oar and dreams of his freedom, till the lash of the master wakes him.

I myself was that slave, and I dreamed of freedom, but the sleep of my grandfather was upon me. My flesh needed the whip of my own day.

Even in the presence of the Nazarene I had closed my eyes to see my hands chained to the oar. Doubt is a pain too lonely to know that faith is his twin brother.

Doubt is a foundling unhappy and astray, and though his own mother who gave him birth should find him and enfold him, he would withdraw in caution and in fear.

For Doubt will not know truth till his wounds are healed and restored.

I doubted Jesus until He made Himself manifest to me, and thrust my own hand into His very wounds.

Then indeed I believed, and after that I was rid of my yesterday and the yesterdays of my forefathers.

The dead in me buried their dead; and the living shall live for the Anointed King, even for Him who was the Son of Man.

Yesterday they told me that I must go and utter His name among the Persians and the Hindus.

I shall go. And from this day to my last day, at dawn and at eventide, I shall see my Lord rising in majesty and I shall hear Him speak.

ELMADAM THE LOGICIAN

YOU BID ME SPEAK OF JESUS THE NAZARENE, and much have I to tell, but the time has not come. Yet whatever I say of Him now is the truth; for all speech is worthless save when it discloses the truth.

Behold a man disorderly, against all order; a mendicant, opposed to all possessions; a drunkard who would only make merry with rogues and castaways.

He was not the proud son of the State, nor was He the protected citizen of the Empire; therefore He had contempt for both State and Empire.

He would live as free and dutiless as the fowls of the air, and for this the hunters brought Him to earth with arrows.

No man shall ram the towers of yesterday and escape the falling stones.

No one shall open the flood gates of his ancestors without drowning. It is the law. And because that Nazarene broke the law, He and His witless followers were brought to naught.

And there lived many others like Him, men who would change the course of our destiny.

They themselves were changed, and they were the losers.

There is a grapeless vine that grows by the city walls. It creeps upward and clings to the stones. Should that vine say in her heart, "With my might and my weight I shall destroy these walls," what would the other plants say? Surely they would laugh at her foolishness.

Now sir, I cannot but laugh at this man and His ill-advised disciples.

ONE OF THE MARYS

IS HEAD WAS ALWAYS HIGH, AND THE FLAME OF GOD was in His eyes.

He was often sad, but His sadness was tenderness shown to those in pain, and comradeship given to the lonely.

When He smiled His smile was as the hunger of those who long after the unknown. It was like the dust of stars falling upon the eyelids of children. And it was like a morsel of bread in the throat.

He was sad, yet it was a sadness that would rise to the lips and become a smile.

It was like a golden veil in the forest when autumn is upon the world. And sometimes it seemed like moonlight upon the shores of the lake.

He smiled as if His lips would sing at the wedding-feast.

Yet He was sad with the sadness of the winged who will not soar above his comrade.

RUMANOUS

A GREEK POET

HE WAS A POET. HE SAW FOR OUR EYES AND HEARD FOR our ears, and our silent words were upon His lips; and His fingers touched what we could not feel.

Out of His heart there flew countless singing birds to the north and to the south, and the little flowers on the hill-sides stayed His steps towards the heavens.

Oftentimes I have seen Him bending down to touch the blades of grass. And in my heart I have heard Him say: "Little green things, you shall be with me in my kingdom, even as the oaks of Besan, and the cedars of Lebanon."

He loved all things of loveliness, the shy faces of children, and the myrrh and frankincense from the south.

He loved a pomegranate or a cup of wine given Him in kindness; it mattered not whether it was offered by a stranger in the inn or by a rich host.

And He loved the almond blossoms. I have seen Him gathering them into His hands and covering His face with the petals, as though He would embrace with His love all the trees in the world.

He knew the sea and the heavens; and He spoke of pearls which have light that is not of this light, and of stars that are beyond our night.

He knew the mountains as eagles know them, and the valleys as they are known by the brooks and the streams. And there was a desert in His silence and a garden in His speech.

Aye, He was a poet whose heart dwelt in a bower beyond the heights, and His songs though sung for our ears, were sung for other ears also, and to men in another land where life is for ever young and time is always dawn.

Once I too deemed myself a poet, but when I stood before Him in Bethany, I knew what it is to hold an instrument with but a single string before one who commands all instruments. For in His voice there was the laughter of thunder and the tears of rain, and the joyous dancing of trees in the wind.

And since I have known that my lyre has but one string, and that my voice weaves neither the memories of yesterday nor the hopes of tomorrow, I have put aside my lyre and I shall keep silence. But always at twilight I shall hearken, and I shall listen to the Poet who is the sovereign of all poets.

LEVI

A DISCIPLE

UPON AN EVENTIDE HE PASSED BY MY HOUSE, AND MY soul was quickened within me.

He spoke to me and said, "Come, Levi, and follow me."

And I followed Him that day.

And at the eventide of the next day I begged Him to enter my house and be my guest. And He and His friends crossed my threshold and blessed me and my wife and my children.

And I had other guests. They were publicans and men of learning, but they were against Him in their hearts.

And when we were sitting about the board, one of the publicans questioned Jesus, saying, "Is it true that you and your disciples break the law, and make fire on the sabbath day?"

And Jesus answered Him saying, "We do indeed make fire on the sabbath day. We would inflame the sabbath day, and we would burn with our torch the dry stubble of all the days."

And another publican said, "It was brought to us that you drink wine with the unclean at the inn."

And Jesus answered, "Aye, these also we would comfort. Came we here except to share the loaf and the cup with the uncrowned and the unshod amongst you?

"Few, aye too few are the featherless who dare the wind, and many are the winged and full-fledged yet in the nest.

"And we would feed them all with our beak, both the sluggish and the swift."

And another publican said, "Have I not been told that you would protect the harlots of Jerusalem?"

Then in the face of Jesus I saw, as it were, the rocky heights of Lebanon, and He said, "It is true.

"On the day of reckoning these women shall rise before the throne of my Father, and they shall be made pure by their own tears. But you shall be held down by the chains of your own judgment.

"Babylon was not put to waste by her prostitutes; Babylon fell to ashes that the eyes of her hypocrites might no longer see the light of day."

And other publicans would have questioned Him, but I made a sign and bade them be silent, for I knew He would confound them; and they too were my guests, and I would not have them put to shame.

When it was midnight the publicans left my house, and their souls were limping.

Then I closed my eyes and I saw, as if in a vision, seven women in white raiment standing about Jesus. Their arms were crossed upon their bosoms, and their heads were bent down, and I looked deep into the mist of my dream and beheld the face of one of the seven women, and it shone in my darkness.

It was the face of a harlot who lived in Jerusalem.

Then I opened my eyes and looked at Him, and He was smiling at me and at the others who had not left the board.

And I closed my eyes again, and I saw in a light seven men in white garments standing around Him. And I beheld the face of one of them.

It was the face of the thief who was crucified afterward at His right hand.

And later Jesus and His comrades left my house for the road.

A WIDOW IN GALILEE

MY SON WAS MY FIRST AND MY ONLY BORN. He labored in our field and he was Contented until he heard the man called Jesus speaking to the multitude.

Then my son suddenly became different, as if a new spirit, foreign and unwholesome, had embraced his spirit.

He abandoned the field and the garden; and he abandoned me also. He became worthless, a creature of the highways.

That man Jesus of Nazareth was evil, for what good man would separate a son from his mother?

The last thing my child said to me was this:

I am going with one of His disciples to the North Country. My life is established upon the Nazarene. You have given me birth, and for that I am grateful to you. But I needs must go. Am I not leaving with you our rich land, and all our silver and gold? I shall take naught but this garment and this staff."

Thus my son spoke, and departed.

And now the Romans and the priests have laid hold upon Jesus and crucified Him; and they have done well.

A man who would part mother and son could not be godly. The man who sends our children to the cities of the Gentiles cannot be our friend.

I know my son will not return to me. I saw it in his eyes. And for this I hate Jesus of Nazareth who caused me to be alone in this unploughed field and this withered garden.

And I hate all those who praise Him.

Not many days ago they told me that Jesus once said, "My father and my mother and my brethren are those who hear my word and follow me."

But why should sons leave their mothers to follow His footsteps?

And why should the milk of my breast be forgotten for a fountain not yet tasted? And the warmth of my arms be forsaken for the Northland, cold and unfriendly?

Aye, I hate the Nazarene, and I shall hate Him to the end of my days, for He has robbed me of my first-born, my only son.

JUDAS

THE COUSIN OF JESUS

UPON A NIGHT IN THE MONTH OF AUGUST we were with the Master on a heath not far from the lake. The heath was called by the ancients the Meadow of Skulls.

And Jesus was reclining on the grass and gazing at the stars.

And of a sudden two men came rushing towards us breathless. They were as if in agony, and they fell prostrate at the feet of Jesus.

And Jesus stood up and He said, "Whence came you?"

And one of the men answered, "From Machaereus."

And Jesus looked upon him and was troubled, and He said, "What of John?"

And the man said, "He was slain this day. He was beheaded in his prison cell."

Then Jesus lifted up His head. And then He walked a little way from us. After a while He stood again in our midst.

And He said, "The king could have slain the prophet ere this day. Verily the king has tried the pleasure of His subjects. Kings of yore were not so slow in giving the head of a prophet to the headhunters. "I grieve not for John, but rather for Herod, who let fall the sword. Poor king, like an animal caught and led with a ring and a rope.

"Poor petty tetrarchs lost in their own darkness, they stumble and fall down. And what would you of the stagnant sea but dead fishes?

"I hate not kings. Let them rule men, but only when they are wiser than men."

And the Master looked at the two sorrowful faces and then He looked at us, and He spoke again and said, "John was born wounded, and the blood of his wound streamed forth with his words. He was freedom not yet free from itself, and patient only with the straight and the just.

"In truth he was a voice crying in the land of the deaf; and I loved him in his pain and his aloneness.

"And I loved his pride that would give its head to the sword ere it would yield it to the dust.

"Verily I say unto you that John, the son of Zachariah, was the last of his race, and like his forefathers he was slain between the threshold of the temple and the altar."

And again Jesus walked away from us.

Then He returned and He said, "Forever it has been that those who rule for an hour would slay the rulers of years. And forever they would hold a trial and pronounce condemnation upon a man not yet born, and decree his death ere he commits the crime.

"The son of Zachariah shall live with me in my kingdom and his day shall be long."

Then He turned to the disciples of John and said, "Every deed has its morrow. I myself may be the morrow of this deed. Go back to my friend's friends, and tell them I shall be with them."

And the two men walked away from us, and they seemed less heavy-hearted.

Then Jesus laid Himself down again upon the grass and outstretched His arms, and again He gazed at the stars.

Now it was late. And I lay not far from Him, and I would fain have rested, but there was a hand knocking upon the gate of my sleep, and I lay awake until Jesus and the dawn called me again to the road.

THE MAN FROM THE DESERT

I WAS A STRANGER IN JERUSALEM. I HAD COME TO the Holy City to behold the great temple, and to sacrifice upon the altar, for my wife had given twin sons to my tribe.

And after I had made my offering, I stood in the portico of the temple looking down upon the money-changers and those who sold doves for sacrifice, and listening to the great noise in the court.

And as I stood there came of a sudden a man into the midst of the money-changers and those who sold doves.

He was a man of majesty, and He came swiftly.

In His hand He held a rope of goat's hide; and He began to overturn the tables of the money-changers and to beat the pedlars of birds with the rope.

And I heard Him saying with a loud voice, "Render these birds unto the sky which is their nest."

Men and women fled from before His face, and He moved amongst them as the whirling wind moves on the sand-hills.

All this came to pass in but a moment, and then the court of the Temple was emptied of the money-changers. Only the man stood there alone, and His followers stood at a distance. Then I turned my face and I saw another man in the portico of the temple. And I walked towards him and said, "Sir, who is this man who stands alone, even like another temple?" And he answered me, "This is Jesus of Nazareth, a prophet who has appeared of late in Galilee. Here in Jerusalem all men hate Him."

And I said, "My heart was strong enough to be with His whip, and yielding enough to be at His feet."

And Jesus turned towards His followers who were awaiting Him. But before He reached them, three of the temple doves flew back, and one alighted upon His left shoulder and the other two at His feet. And He touched each one tenderly. Then He walked on, and there were leagues in every step of His steps.

Now tell me, what power had He to attack and disperse hundreds of men and women without opposition? I was told that they all hate Him, yet no one stood before Him on that day. Had He plucked out the fangs of hate on His way to the court of the temple?

PETER

ONCE AT SUNDOWN JESUS LED US INTO THE village of Bethsaida. We were a tired company, and the dust of the road was upon us.

And we came to a great house in the midst of a garden, and the owner stood at the gate.

And Jesus said to him, "These men are weary and footsore. Let them sleep in your house. The night is cold and they are in need of warmth and rest."

And the rich man said, "They shall not sleep in my house."

And Jesus said, "Suffer them then to sleep in your garden."

And the man answered, "Nay, they shall not sleep in my garden."

Then Jesus turned to us and said, "This is what your tomorrow will be, and this present is like your future. All doors shall be closed in your face, and not even the gardens that lie under the stars may be your couch.

"Should your feet indeed be patient with the road and follow me, it may be you will find a basin and a bed, and perhaps bread and wine also. But if it should be that you find none of these things, forget not then that you have crossed one of my deserts. Come, let us go forth." And the rich man was disturbed, and his face was changed, and he muttered to himself words that I did not hear; and he shrank away from us and turned into his garden.

And we followed Jesus upon the road.

MELACHI OF BABYLON

AN ASTRONOMER

YOU QUESTION ME CONCERNING THE MIRACLES OF JESUS. Every thousand thousand years the sun and the moon and this earth and all her sister planets meet in a straight line, and they confer for a moment together.

Then they slowly disperse and await the passing of another thousand thousand years.

There are no miracles beyond the seasons, yet you and I do not know all the seasons. And what if a season shall be made manifest in the shape of a man?

In Jesus the elements of our bodies and our dreams came together according to law. All that was timeless before Him became timeful in Him.

They say He gave sight to the blind and walking to the paralysed, and that He drove devils out of madmen.

Perchance blindness is but a dark thought that can be overcome by a burning thought. Perchance a withered limb is but idleness that can be quickened by energy. And perhaps the devils, these restless elements in our life, are driven out by the angels of peace and serenity.

They say He raised the dead to life. If you can tell me WHAT IS DEATH, then I will tell you WHAT IS LIFE.

In a field I have watched an acorn, a thing so still and seemingly useless. And in the spring I have seen that acorn take roots and rise, the beginning of an oak tree, towards the sun.

Surely you would deem this a miracle, yet that miracle is wrought a thousand thousand times in the drowsiness of every autumn and the passion of every spring.

Why shall it not be wrought in the heart of man? Shall not the seasons meet in the hand or upon the lips of a Man Anointed?

If our God has given to earth the art to nestle seed whilst the seed is seemingly dead, why shall He not give to the heart of man to breathe life into another heart, even a heart seemingly dead?

I have spoken of these miracles which I deem but little beside the greater miracle, which is the man Himself, the Wayfarer, the man who turned my dross into gold, who taught me how to love those who hate me, and in so doing brought me comfort and gave sweet dreams to my sleep.

This is the miracle in my own life.

My soul was blind, my soul was lame. I was possessed by restless spirits, and I was dead.

But now I see clearly, and I walk erect. I am at peace, and I live to witness and proclaim my own being every hour of the day.

And I am not one of His followers. I am but an old astronomer who visits the fields of space once a season, and who would be heedful of the law and the miracles thereof.

And I am at the twilight of my time, but whenever I would seek its dawning, I seek the youth of Jesus.

And for ever shall age seek youth. In me now it is knowledge that is seeking vision.

A PHILOSOPHER

WHEN HE WAS WITH US HE GAZED AT US AND AT OUR world with eyes of wonder, for His eyes were not veiled with the veil of years, and all that He saw was clear in the light of His youth.

Though He knew the depth of beauty, He was for ever surprised by its peace and its majesty; and He stood before the earth as the first man had stood before the first day.

We whose senses have been dulled, we gaze in full daylight and yet we do not see. We would cup our ears, but we do not hear; and stretch forth our hands, but we do not touch. And though all the incense of Arabia is burned, we go our way and do not smell.

We see not the ploughman returning from his field at eventide; nor hear the shepherd's flute when he leads his flock to the fold; nor do we stretch our arms to touch the sunset; and our nostrils hunger no longer for the roses of Sharon.

Nay, we honor no kings without kingdoms; nor hear the sound of harps save when the strings are plucked by hands; nor do we see a child playing in our olive grove as if he were a young olive tree. And all words must needs rise from lips of flesh, or else we deem each other dumb and deaf. In truth we gaze but do not see, and hearken but do not hear; we eat and drink but do not taste. And there lies the difference between Jesus of Nazareth and ourselves.

His senses were all continually made new, and the world to Him was always a new world.

To Him the lisping of a babe was not less than the cry of all mankind, while to us it is only lisping.

To Him the root of a buttercup was a longing towards God, while to us it is naught but a root.

URIAH

AN OLD MAN OF NAZARETH

HE WAS A STRANGER IN OUR MIDST, AND HIS LIFE WAS hidden with dark veils.

He walked not the path of our God, but followed the course of the foul and the infamous.

His childhood revolted, and rejected the sweet milk of our nature.

His youth was inflamed like dry grass that burns in the night.

And when He became man, He took arms against us all.

Such men are conceived in the ebb tide of human kindness, and born in unholy tempests. And in tempests they live a day and then perish forever.

Do you not remember Him, a boy overweening, who would argue with our learned elders, and laugh at their dignity?

And remember you not His youth, when He lived by the saw and the chisel? He would not accompany our sons and daughters on their holidays. He would walk alone.

And He would not return the salutation of those who hailed Him, as though He were above us.

I myself met Him once in the field and greeted Him, and He only smiled, and in His smile I beheld arrogance and insult. Not long afterward my daughter went with her companions to the vineyards to gather the grapes, and she too spoke to Him and He did not answer her.

He spoke only to the whole company of grape-gatherers, as if my daughter had not been among them.

When He abandoned His people and turned vagabond He became naught but a babbler. His voice was like a claw in our flesh, and the sound of His voice is still a pain in our memory.

He would utter only evil of us and of our fathers and forefathers. And His tongue sought our bosoms like a poisoned arrow.

Such was Jesus.

If He had been my son, I would have committed Him with the Roman legions to Arabia, and I would have begged the captain to place Him in the forefront of the battle, so that the archer of the foe might mark Him, and free me of His insolence.

But I have no son. And mayhap I should be grateful. For what if my son had been an enemy of his own people, and my gray hairs were now seeking the dust with shame, my white beard humbled?

NICODEMUS THE POET

THE YOUNGEST OF THE ELDERS

IN THE SANHEDRIM

MANY ARE THE FOOLS WHO SAY THAT JESUS stood in His own path and opposed Himself; that He knew not His own mind, and in the absence of that knowledge confounded Himself.

Many indeed are the owls who know no song unlike their own hooting.

You and I know the jugglers of words who would honor only a greater juggler, men who carry their heads in baskets to the market-place and sell them to the first bidder.

We know the pygmies who abuse the sky-man. And we know what the weed would say of the oak tree and the cedar.

I pity them that they cannot rise to the heights.

I pity the shrivelling thorn envying the elm that dares the seasons.

But pity, though enfolded by the regret of all the angels, can bring them no light.

I know the scarecrow whose rotting garments flutter in the corn, yet he himself is dead to the corn and to the singing wind. I know the wingless spider that weaves a net for all who fly.

I know the crafty, the blowers of horns and the beaters of drums, who in the abundance of their own noise cannot hear the skylark nor the east wind in the forest.

I know him who paddles against all streams, but never finds the source, who runs with all rivers, but never dares to the sea.

I know him who offers his unskilled hands to the builder of the temple, and when his unskilled hands are rejected, says in the darkness of his heart,

I will destroy all that shall be builded."

I know all these. They are the men who object that Jesus said on a certain day, "I bring peace unto you," and on another day, "I bring a sword."

They cannot understand that in truth he said, "I bring peace unto men of goodwill, and I lay a sword between him who would peace and him who would a sword."

They wonder that He who said, "My kingdom is not of this earth," said also, "Render unto Caesar that which is Caesar's "; and know not that if they would indeed be free to enter the kingdom of their passion, they must not resist the gate-keeper of their necessities. It behooves them gladly to pay that dole to enter into that city.

"These are the men who say, "He preached tenderness and kindliness and filial love, yet He would not heed His mother and His brothers when they sought Him in the streets of Jerusalem."

They do not know that His mother and brothers in their loving fear would have had Him return to the bench of the carpenter, whereas He was opening our eyes to the dawn of a new day.

His mother and His brothers would have had Him live in the shadow of death, but He Himself was challenging death upon yonder hill that He might live in our sleepless memory.

I know these moles that dig paths to nowhere. Are they not the ones who accuse Jesus of glorifying Himself in that He said to the multitude, "I am the path and the gate to salvation," and even called Himself the life and the resurrection.

But Jesus was not claiming more than the month of May claims in her high tide.

Was He not to tell the shining truth because it was so shining?

He indeed said that He was the way and the life and the resurrection of the heart; and I myself am a testimony to His truth.

Do you not remember me, Nicodemus, who believed in naught but the laws and decrees and was in continual subjection to observances?

And behold me now, a man who walks with life and laughs with the sun from the first moment it smiles upon the mountain until it yields itself to bed behind the hills. Why do you halt before the word salvation? I myself through Him have attained my salvation.

I care not for what shall befall me tomorrow, for I know that Jesus quickened my sleep and made my distant dreams my companions and my roadfellows.

Am I less man because I believe in a greater man?

The barriers of flesh and bone fell down when the Poet of Galilee spoke to me; and I was held by a spirit, and was lifted to the heights, and in midair my wings gathered the song of passion.

And when I dismounted from the wind and in the Sanhedrim my pinions were shorn, even then my ribs, my featherless wings, kept and guarded the song. And all the poverties of the lowlands cannot rob me of my treasure.

I have said enough. Let the deaf bury the humming of life in their dead ears. I am content with the sound of His lyre, which He held and struck while the hands of His body were nailed and bleeding.

JOSEPH OF ARIMATMEA

TEN YEARS AFTER

HERE WERE TWO STREAMS RUNNING IN THE heart of the Nazarene: the stream of kinship to God whom He called Father, and the stream of rapture which He called the kingdom of the Above-world.

And in my solitude I thought of Him and I followed these two streams in His heart. Upon the banks of the one I met my own soul; and sometimes my soul was a beggar and a wanderer, and sometimes it was a princess in her garden.

Then I followed the other stream in His heart, and on my way I met one who had been beaten and robbed of his gold, and he was smiling. And farther on I saw the robber who had robbed him, and there were unshed tears upon his face.

Then I heard the murmur of these two streams in my own bosom also, and I was gladdened.

When I visited Jesus the day before Pontius Pilatus and the elders laid hands on Him, we talked long, and I asked Him many questions, and He answered my questionings with graciousness; and when I left Him I knew He was the Lord and Master of this our earth.

It is long since the cedar tree has fallen, but its fragrance endures, and will forever seek the four corners of the earth.

GEORGUS OF BEIRUT

HE AND HIS FRIENDS WERE IN THE GROVE of pines beyond my hedge, and He was talking to them.

I stood near the hedge and listened. And I knew who He was, for His fame had reached these shores ere He Himself visited them.

When He ceased speaking I approached Him, and I said, "Sir, come with these men and honor me and my roof."

And He smiled upon me and said, "Not this day, my friend. Not this day."

And there was a blessing in His words, and His voice enfolded me like a garment on a cold night.

Then He turned to His friends and said, "Behold a man who deems us not strangers, and though He has not seen us ere this day, he bids us to His threshold.

"Verily in my kingdom there are no strangers. Our life is but the life of all other men, given us that we may know all men, and in that knowledge love them.

"The deeds of all men are but our deeds, both the hidden and the revealed.

"I charge you not to be one self but rather many selves, the householder and the homeless, the ploughman and the sparrow that picks the grain ere it slumber in the earth, the giver who gives in gratitude, and the receiver who receives in pride and recognition.

"The beauty of the day is not only in what you see, but in what other men see.

"For this I have chosen you from among the many who have chosen me."

Then He turned to me again and smiled and said, "I say these things to you also, and you also shall remember them."

Then I entreated Him and said, "Master, will you not visit in my house?"

And He answered, "I know your heart, and I have visited your larger house."

And as He walked away with His disciples He said, "Good-night, and may your house be large enough to shelter all the wanderers of the land."

MARY MAGDALEN

HIS MOUTH WAS LIKE THE HEART OF A POMEGRANATE, and the shadows in His eyes were deep.

And He was gentle, like a man mindful of his own strength.

In my dreams I beheld the kings of the earth standing in awe in His presence.

I would speak of His face, but how shall I?

It was like night without darkness, and like day without the noise of day.

It was a sad face, and it was a joyous face.

And well I remember how once He raised His hand towards the sky, and His parted fingers were like the branches of an elm.

And I remember Him pacing the evening. He was not walking. He Himself was a road above the road; even as a cloud above the earth that would descend to refresh the earth.

But when I stood before Him and spoke to Him, He was a man, and His face was powerful to behold. And He said to me, "What would you, Miriam?"

I did not answer Him, but my wings enfolded my secret, and I was made warm. And because I could bear His light no more, I turned and walked away, but not in shame. I was only shy, and I would be alone, with His fingers upon the strings of my heart.

JOTHAM OF NAZARETH

TO A ROMAN

MY FRIEND, YOU LIKE ALL OTHER ROMANS would conceive life rather than live it. You would rule lands rather than be ruled by the spirit.

You would conquer races and be cursed by them rather than stay in Rome and be blest and happy

You think but of armies marching and of ships launched into the sea.

How shall you then understand Jesus of Nazareth, a man simple and alone, who came without armies or ships, to establish a kingdom in the heart and an empire in the free spaces of the soul?

How shall you understand this man who was not a warrior, but who came with the power of the mighty ether?

He was not a god, He was a man like unto ourselves; but in Him the myrrh of the earth rose to meet the frankincense of the sky; and in His words our lisping embraced the whispering of the unseen; and in His voice we heard a song unfathomable.

Aye, Jesus was a man and not a god, and therein lies our wonder and our surprise.

But you Romans wonder not save at the gods, and no man shall surprise you. Therefore you understand not the Nazarene.

He belonged to the youth of the mind and you belong to its old age.

You govern us today; but let us wait another day.

Who knows but that this man with neither armies nor ships shall govern tomorrow?

We who follow the spirit shall sweat blood while journeying after Him. But Rome shall lie a white skeleton in the sun.

We shall suffer much, yet we shall endure and we shall live. But Rome must needs fall into the dust.

Yet if Rome, when humbled and made low, shall pronounce His name, He will heed her voice. And He will breathe new life into her bones that she may rise again, a city among the cities of the earth.

But this He shall do without legions, nor with slaves to oar His galleys. He will be alone.

EPHRAIM OF JERICHO

WHEN HE CAME AGAIN TO JERICHO sought Him out and said to Him, "Master, on the morrow my son will take a wife. I beg you come to the wedding-feast and do us honor, even as you honored the wedding at Cana of Galilee."

And He answered, "It is true that I was once a guest at a wedding-feast, but I shall not be a guest again. I am myself now the Bridegroom."

And I said, "I entreat you, Master, come to the wedding-feast of my son."

And He smiled as though He would rebuke me, and said, "Why Go you entreat me? Have you not wine enough?"

And I said, "My jugs are full, Master; yet I beseech you, come to my son's wedding-feast."

Then He said, "Who knows? I may come, I may surely come, if your heart is an altar in your temple."

Upon the morrow my son was married, but Jesus came not to the wedding-feast. And though we had many guests, I felt that no one had come.

In very truth, I myself who welcomed the guests, was not there.

Perhaps my heart had not been an altar when I invited Him. Perhaps I desired another miracle.

BARCA

A MERCHANT OF TYRE

I BELIEVE THAT NEITHER THE ROMANS NOR THE JEWS understood Jesus of Nazareth, nor did His disciples who now preach His name.

The Romans slew Him and that was a blunder. The Galileans would make a god of Him and that is a mistake.

Jesus was of the heart of man.

I have sailed the Seven Seas with my ships, and bartered with kings and princes and with cheats and the wily in the market-places of distant cities; but never have I seen a man who understood merchants as He did.

I heard Him once tell this parable:

"A merchant left his country for a foreign land. He had two servants, and he gave each a handful of gold, saying: 'Even as I go abroad, you also shall go forth and seek profit. Make just exchange, and see that you serve in giving and taking.'

And after a year the merchant returned.

And he asked his two servants what they had done with his gold.

"The first servant said, 'Behold, Master, I have bought and sold, and I have gained.'

"And the merchant answered, 'The gain shall be yours, for you have done well, and have been faithful to me and to yourself.'

"Then the other servant stood forth and said, "Sir, I feared the loss of your money; and I did not buy nor sell. Behold, it is all here in this purse.'

"And the merchant took the gold, and said, 'Little is your faith. To barter and lose is better than not to go forth. For even as the wind scatters her seed and waits for the fruit, so must all merchants. It were fitter for you henceforth to serve others.'"

When Jesus spoke thus, though He was no merchant, He disclosed the secret of commerce.

Moreover, His parables often brought to my mind lands more distant than my journeys, and yet nearer than my house and my goods.

But the young Nazarene was not a god; and it is a pity His followers seek to make a god of such a sage.

PHUMIAH

THE HIGH PRIESTESS OF SIDON

TO THE OTHER PRIESTESSES

TAKE YOUR HARPS AND LET ME SING.
Beat your strings, the silver and the gold;
For I would sing the dauntless Man
Who slew the dragon of the valley,
Then gazed down with pity
Upon the thing He had slain.

Take your harps and sing with me
The lofty Oak upon the height,
The sky-hearted and the ocean-handed Man,
Who kissed the pallid lips of death,
Yet quivers now upon the mouth of life.

Take your harps and let us sing
The fearless Hunter on the hill,
Who marked the beast, and shot His viewless arrow,
And brought the horn and tusk
Down to the earth.

Take your harps and sing with me
The valiant Youth who conquered the mountain cities,
And the cities of the plain that coiled like serpents in the sand.
He fought not against pygmies but against gods
Who hungered for our flesh and thirsted for our blood.

And like the first Golden Hawk
He would rival only eagles;
For His wings were vast and proud
And would not outwing the less winged.

Take your harps and sing with me
The joyous song of sea and cliff.
The gods are dead,
And they are lying still
In the forgotten isle of a forgotten sea.
And He who slew them sits upon His throne.

He was but a youth.
Spring had not yet given Him full beard,

And His summer was still young in His field.

Take your harps and sing with me
The tempest in the forest
That breaks the dry branch and the leafless twig,
Yet sends the living root to nestle deeper at the breast of earth.

Take your harps and sing with me
The deathless song of our Beloved.
Nay, my maidens, stay your hands.
Lay by your harps.
We cannot sing Him now.
The faint whisper of our song cannot reach His tempest,
Nor pierce the majesty of His silence.

Lay by your harps and gather close around me,
I would repeat His words to you,
And I would tell you of His deeds,
For the echo of His voice is deeper than our passion.

BENJAMIN THE SCRIBE

IT HAS BEEN SAID THAT JESUS WAS THE ENEMY OF Rome and Judea.

But I say that Jesus was the enemy of no man and no race.

I have heard Him say, "The birds of the air and the mountain tops are not mindful of the serpents in their dark holes.

"Let the dead bury their dead. Be you yourself among the living, and soar high."

I was not one of His disciples. I was but one of the many who went after Him to gaze at His face.

He looked upon Rome and upon us who are the slaves of Rome, as a father looks upon his children playing with toys and fighting among themselves for the larger toy. And He laughed from His height.

He was greater than State and race; He was greater than revolution.

He was single and alone, and He was an awakening.

He wept all our unshed tears and smiled all our revolts.

We knew it was in His power to be born with all who are not yet born, and to bid them see, not with their eyes but with His vision. Jesus was the beginning of a new kingdom upon the earth, and that kingdom shall remain.

He was the son and the grandson of all the kings who builded the kingdom of the spirit.

And only the kings of spirit have ruled our world.

ZACCHAEUS

YOU BELIEVE IN WHAT YOU HEAR SAID. Believe in the unsaid, for the silence of men is nearer the truth than their words.

You ask if Jesus could have escaped His shameful death and saved His followers from persecution.

I answer, He could indeed have escaped had He chosen, but He did not seek safety nor was He mindful of protecting His flock from wolves of the night.

He knew His fate and the morrow of His constant lovers. He foretold and prophesied what should befall every one of us. He sought not His death; but He accepted death as a husbandman shrouding his corn with earth, accepts the winter, and then awaits the spring and harvest; and as a builder lays the largest stone in the foundation.

We were men of Galilee and from the slopes of Lebanon. Our Master could have led us back to our country, to live with His youth in our gardens until old age should come and whisper us back into the years.

Was anything barring His path back to the temples of our villages where others were reading the prophets and then disclosing their hearts? Could He not have said, "Now I go east with the west wind," and so saying dismiss us with a smile upon His lips?

Aye, He could have said, "Go back to your kin. The world is not ready for me. I shall return a thousand years hence. Teach your children to await my return."

He could have done this had He so chosen.

But He knew that to build the temple invisible He must needs lay Himself the corner-stone, and lay us around as little pebbles cemented close to Himself.

He knew that the sap of His sky-tree must rise from its roots, and He poured His blood upon its roots; and to Him it was not sacrifice but rather gain.

Death is the revealer. The death of Jesus revealed His life.

Had He escaped you and His enemies, you would have been the conquerors of the world. Therefore He did not escape.

Only He who desires all shall give all.

Aye, Jesus could have escaped His enemies and lived to old age. But He knew the passing of the seasons, and He would sing His song.

What man facing the armed world would not be conquered for the moment that he might overcome the ages?

And now you ask who, in very truth, slew Jesus, the Romans or the priests of Jerusalem?

Neither the Romans slew Him, nor the priests. The whole world stood to honor Him upon that hill.

JONATHAN

UPON A DAY MY BELOVED AND I WERE ROWING UPON the lake of sweet waters. And the hills of Lebanon were about us.

We moved beside the weeping willows, and the reflections of the willows were deep around us.

And while I steered the boat with an oar, my beloved took her lute and sang thus:

What flower save the lotus knows the waters and the sun? What heart save the lotus heart shall know both earth and sky? Behold my love, the golden flower that floats 'twixt deep and high Even as you and I float betwixt a love that has for ever been And shall for ever be. Dip your oar, my love, And let me touch my strings. Let us follow the willows, and let us leave not the water-lilies. In Nazareth there lives a Poet, and His heart is like the lotus. He has visited the soul of woman, He knows her thirst growing out of the waters, And her hunger for the sun, though all her lips are fed. They say He walks in Galilee. I say He is rowing with us. Can you not see His face, my love? Can you not see, where the willow bough and its reflection meet, He is moving as we move?

Beloved, it is good to know the youth of life.
It is good to know its singing joy.
Would that you might always have the oar,
And I my stringed lute,
Where the lotus laughs in the sun,
And the willow is dipping to the waters,
And His voice is upon my strings.

Dip your oar, my beloved,
And let me touch my strings.
There is a Poet in Nazareth
Who knows and loves us both.
Dip your oar, my lover,
And let me touch my strings.

HANNAH OF BETHSAIDA

THE YEAR 73

THE SISTER OF MY FATHER HAD LEFT US IN her youth to dwell in a hut beside her father's ancient vineyard.

She lived alone, and the people of the countryside sought her in their maladies, and she healed them with green herbs, and with roots and flowers dried in the sun.

And they deemed her a seeress; but there were those also who called her witch and sorceress.

One day my father said to me, "Take these loaves of wheaten bread to my sister, and take this jug of wine and this basket of raisins."

And it was all put upon the back of a colt, and I followed the road until I reached the vineyard, and the hut of my father's sister. And she was gladdened.

Now as we sat together in the cool of the day, a man came by upon the road, and He greeted the sister of my father, saying: "Good-even to you, and the blessing of the night be upon you."

Then she rose up; and she stood as in awe before Him and said, "Good-even to you, master of all good spirits, and conqueror of all evil spirits."

The man looked at her with tender eyes, and then He passed on by. But I laughed in my heart. Me thought my father's sister was mad. But now I know that she was not mad. It was I who did not understand.

She knew of my laughter, though it was hidden.

And she spoke, but not in anger. She said, "Listen, my daughter, and hearken and keep my word in remembrance: the man who but now passed by, like the shadow of a bird flying between the sun and the earth, shall prevail against the Caesars and the empire of the Caesars. He shall wrestle with the crowned bull of Chaldea, and the man-headed lion of Egypt, and He shall overcome them; and He shall rule the world.

"But this land that now He walks shall come to naught; and Jerusalem, which sits proudly upon the hill, shall drift away in smoke upon the wind of desolation."

When she spoke thus, my laughter turned to stillness and I was quiet. Then I said, "Who is this man, and of what country and tribe does He come? And how shall He conquer the great kings and the empires of the great kings?"

And she answered, "He is one born here in this land, but we have conceived Him in our longing from the beginning of years. He is of all tribes and yet of none. He shall conquer by the word of His mouth and by the flame of His spirit."

Then suddenly she rose and stood up like a pinnacle of rock; and she said, "May the angel of the Lord forgive me for pronouncing this word also: He shall be slain, and His youth shall be shrouded, and He shall be laid in silence beside the tongueless heart of the earth. And the maidens of Judea shall weep for Him."

Then she lifted her hand skyward and spoke again, and she said, "But He shall be slain only in the body.

"In the spirit He shall rise and go forth leading His host from this land where the sun is born, to the land where the sun is slain at eventide.

"And His name shall be first among men."

She was an aged seeress when she said these things, and I was but a girl, a field unploughed, a stone not yet in a wall.

But all that she beheld in the mirror of her mind has come to pass even in my day.

Jesus of Nazareth rose from the dead and led men and women unto the people of the sunset. The city that yielded Him to judgment was given unto destruction; and in the Judgment Hall where He was tried and sentenced, the owl hoots a dirge while the night weeps the dew of her heart upon the fallen marble.

And I am an old woman, and the years bend me down. My people are no more and my race is vanished.

I saw Him but once again after that day, and once again heard His voice. It was upon a hill-top when He was talking to His friends and followers.

And now I am old and alone, yet still He visits my dreams.

He comes like a white angel with pinions; and with His grace He hushes my dread of darkness. And He uplifts me to dreams yet more distant.

I am still a field unploughed, a ripe fruit that would not fall. The most that I possess is the warmth of the sun, and the memory of that man.

I know that among my people there shall not rise again king nor prophet nor priest, even as the sister of my father foretold.

We shall pass with the flowing of the rivers, and we shall be nameless.

But those who crossed Him in mid-stream shall be remembered for crossing Him in mid-stream.

MANASSEH,

A LAWYER IN JERUSALEM

YES, I USED TO HEAR HIM SPEAK. THERE was always a ready word upon His lips.

But I admired Him as a man rather than as a leader. He preached something beyond my liking, perhaps beyond my reason. And I would have no man preach to me.

I was taken by His voice and His gestures, but not by the substance of His speech. He charmed me but never convinced me; for He was too vague, too distant and obscure to reach my mind.

I have known other men like Him. They are never constant nor are they consistent. It is with eloquence not with principles that they hold your ear and your passing thought, but never the core of your heart.

What a pity that His enemies confronted Him and forced the issue. It was not necessary. I believe their hostility will add to His stature and turn His mildness to power.

For is it not strange that in opposing a man you give Him courage? And in staying His feet you give Him wings?

I know not His enemies, yet I am certain that in their fear of a harmless man they have lent Him strength and made Him dangerous.

JEPHTHA OF CAESAREA

THIS MAN WHO FILLS YOUR DAY AND HAUNTS your night is repellent to me. Yet you would tire my ears with His sayings and my mind with His deeds.

I am weary of His words, and all that He did. His very name off ends me, and the name of His countryside. I will none of Him.

Why make you a prophet of a man who was but a shadow? Why see a tower in this sand-dune, or imagine a lake in the raindrops gathered together in this hoof-print?

I scorn not the echo of caves in valleys nor the long shadows of the sunset; but I would not listen to the deceptions that hum in your head, nor study the reflections in your eyes.

What word did Jesus utter that Halliel had not spoken? What wisdom did He reveal that was not of Gamaliel? What are His lispings to the voice of Philo? What cymbals did He beat that were not beaten ere ever He lived?

I hearken to the echo from the caves into the silent valleys, and I gaze upon the long shadows of sunset; but I would not have this man's heart echo the sound of another heart, nor would I have a shadow of the seers call himself a prophet. What man shall speak since Isaiah has spoken? Who dares sing since David? And shall wisdom be born now, after Solomon has been gathered to his fathers?

And what of our prophets, whose tongues were swords and their lips flames?

Left they a straw behind for this gleaner of Galilee? Or a fallen fruit for the beggar from the North Country? There was naught for Him save to break the loaf already baked by our ancestors, and to pour the wine which their holy feet had already pressed from the grapes of old.

It is the potter's hand I honor not the man who buys the ware.

I honor those who sit at the loom rather than the boor who wears the cloth.

Who was this Jesus of Nazareth, and what is He? A man who dared not live His mind. Therefore He faded into oblivion and that is His end.

I beg you, charge not my ears with His words or His deeds. My heart is overfull with the prophets of old, and that is enough.

JOHN THE BELOVED DISCIPLE

IN HIS OLD AGE

YOU WOULD HAVE ME SPEAK OF JESUS, BUT how can I lure the passion-song of the world into a hollowed reed?

In every aspect of the day Jesus was aware of the Father. He beheld Him in the clouds and in the shadows of the clouds that pass over the earth. He saw the Father's face reflected in the quiet pools, and the faint print of His feet upon the sand; and He often closed His eyes to gaze into the Holy Eyes.

The night spoke to Him with the voice of the Father, and in solitude He heard the angel of the Lord calling to Him. And when He stilled Himself to sleep He heard the whispering of the heavens in His dreams.

He was often happy with us, and He would call us brothers.

Behold, He who was the first Word called us brothers, though we were but syllables uttered yesterday.

You ask why I call Him the first Word.

Listen, and I will answer:

In the beginning God moved in space, and out of His measureless stirring the earth was born and the seasons thereof.

Then God moved again, and life streamed forth, and the longing of life sought the height and the depth and would have more of itself.

Then God spoke, and His words were man, and man was a spirit begotten by God's Spirit.

And when God spoke thus, the Christ was His first Word and that Word was perfect; and when Jesus of Nazareth came to the world the first Word was uttered unto us and the sound was made flesh and blood.

Jesus the Anointed was the first Word of God uttered unto man, even as if an apple tree in an orchard should bud and blossom a day before the other trees. And in God's orchard that day was an aeon.

We are all sons and daughters of the Most High, but the Anointed One was His first-born, who dwelt in the body of Jesus of Nazareth, and He walked among us and we beheld Him.

All this I say that you may understand not only in the mind but rather in the spirit. The mind weighs and measures but it is the spirit that reaches the heart of life and embraces the secret; and the seed of the spirit is deathless.

The wind may blow and then cease, and the sea shall swell and then weary, but the heart of life is a sphere quiet and serene, and the star that shines therein is fixed for evermore.

MANNUS THE POMPEIIAN

TO A GREEK

THE JEWS, LIKE THEIR NEIGHBOURS THE Phoenicians and the Arabs, will not suffer their gods to rest for a moment upon the wind.

They are over-thoughtful of their deity, and over-observant of one another's prayer and worship and sacrifice.

While we Romans build marble temples to our gods, these people would discuss their god's nature. When we are in ecstasy we sing and dance round the altars of Jupiter and Juno, of Mars and Venus; but they in their rapture wear sackcloth and cover their heads with ashes-and even lament the day that gave them birth.

And Jesus, the man who revealed God as a being of joy, they tortured Him, and then put Him to death.

These people would not be happy with a happy god. They know only the gods of their pain.

Even Jesus' friends and disciples who knew His mirth and heard His laughter, make an image of His sorrow, and they worship that image.

And in such worship they rise not to their deity; they only bring their deity down to themselves.

I believe however that this philosopher, Jesus, who was not unlike Socrates, will have power over His race and mayhap over other races.

For we are all creatures of sadness and of small doubts. And when a man says to us, "Let us be joyous with the gods," we cannot but heed his voice. Strange that the pain of this man has been fashioned into a rite.

These peoples would discover another Adonis, a god slain in the forest, and they would celebrate his slaying. It is a pity they heed not His laughter.

But let us confess, as Roman to Greek. Do even we ourselves hear the laughter of Socrates in the streets of Athens? Is it ever in us to forget the cup of hemlock, even at the theatre of Dionysus?

Do not rather our fathers still stop at the street corners to chat of troubles and to have a happy moment remembering the doleful end of all our great men?

PONTIUS PILATUS

MY WIFE SPOKE OF HIM MANY TIMES ERE HE WAS brought before me, but I was not concerned.

My wife is a dreamer, and she is given, like so many Roman women of her rank, to Eastern cults and rituals. And these cults are dangerous to the Empire; and when they find a path to the hearts of our women they become destructive.

Egypt came to an end when the Hyksos of Arabia brought to her the one God of their desert. And Greece was overcome and fell to dust when Ashtarte and her seven maidens came from the Syrian shores.

As for Jesus, I never saw the man before He was delivered up to me as a malefactor, as an enemy of His own nation and also of Rome.

He was brought into the Hall of Judgment with His arms bound to His body with ropes.

I was sitting upon the dais, and He walked towards me with long, firm steps; then He stood erect and His head was held high.

And I cannot fathom what came over me at that moment; but it was suddenly my desire, though not my will, to rise and go down from the dais and fall before Him. I felt as if Caesar had entered the Hall, a man greater than even Rome herself.

But this lasted only a moment. And then I saw simply a man who was accused of treason by His own people. And I was His governor and His judge.

I questioned Him but He would not answer. He only looked at me. And in His look was pity, as if it were He who was my governor and my judge.

Then there rose from without the cries of the people. But He remained silent, and still He was looking at me with pity in His eyes.

And I went out upon the steps of the palace, and when the people saw me they ceased to cry out. And I said, "What would you with this man?"

And they shouted as if with one throat, "We would crucify Him. He is our enemy and the enemy of Rome."

And some called out, "Did He not say He would destroy the temple? And was it not He who claimed the kingdom? We will have no king but Caesar."

Then I left them and went back into the Judgment Hall again, and I saw Him still standing there alone, and His head was still high.

And I remembered what I had read that a Greek philosopher said: "The lonely man is the strongest man." At that moment the Nazarene was greater than His race. And I did not feel clement towards Him. He was beyond my clemency.

I asked Him then, "Are you the King of the Jews?"

And He said not a word.

And I asked Him again, "Have you not said that you are the King of the Jews?

And He looked upon me.

Then He answered with a quiet voice, "You yourself proclaimed me king. Perhaps to this end I was born, and for this cause came to bear witness unto truth."

Behold a man speaking of truth at such a moment.

In my impatience I said aloud, to myself as much as to Him, "What is truth? And what is truth to the guiltless when the hand of the executioner is already upon him?"

Then Jesus said with power, None shall rule the world save with the Spirit and truth."

And I asked Him saying, "Are you of the Spirit?"

He answered, "So are you also, though you know it not'"

And what was the Spirit and what was truth, when I, for the sake of the State, and they from jealousy for their ancient rites, delivered an innocent man unto His death? No man, no race, no empire would halt before a truth on its way towards self-fulfilment.

And I said again, "Are you the King of the Jews?"

And He answered, "You yourself say this. I have conquered the world ere this hour."

And this alone of all that He said was unseemly, inasmuch as only Rome had conquered the world.

But now the voices of the people rose again, and the noise was greater than before.

And I descended from my seat and said to Him, Follow me."

And again I appeared upon the steps of the palace, and He stood there beside me.

When the people saw Him they roared like the roaring thunder. And in their clamour I heard naught save "Crucify Him, crucify Him."

Then I yielded Him to the priests who had yielded Him to me and I said to them, "Do what you will with this just man. And if it is in your desire, take with you soldiers of Rome to guard Him."

Then they took Him, and I decreed that there be written upon the cross above His head, "Jesus of Nazareth, King of the Jews." I should have said instead, "Jesus of Nazareth, a King."

And the man was stripped and flogged and crucified. It would have been within my power to save Him, but saving Him would have caused a revolution; and it is always wise for the governor of a Roman province not to be intolerant of the religious scruples of a conquered race.

I believe, unto this hour that the man was more than an agitator. What I decreed was not my will, but rather for the sake of Rome.

Not long after, we left Syria, and from that day my wife has been a woman of sorrow. Sometimes even here in this garden I see a tragedy in her face.

I am told she talks much of Jesus to other women of Rome.

Behold, the man whose death I decreed returns from the world of shadows and enters into my own house.

And within myself I ask again and again, What is truth and what is not truth?

Can it be that the Syrian is conquering us in the quiet hours of the night?
It should not indeed be so.
For Rome must needs prevail against the nightmares of our wives.

BARTHOLOMEW IN EPHESUS

THE ENEMIES OF JESUS SAY THAT HE ADDRESSED His appeal to slaves and outcasts, and would have incited them against their lords. They say that because He was of the lowly He invoked His own kind, yet that He sought to conceal His own origin.

But let us consider the followers of Jesus, and His leadership.

In the beginning He chose for companions a few men from the North Country, and they were freemen. They were strong of body and bold of spirit, and in these past two score years they have had the courage to face death with willingness and defiance.

Think you that these men were slaves or outcasts?

And think you that the proud princes of Lebanon and Armenia have forgotten their station in accepting Jesus as a prophet of God?

Or think you the high-born men and women of Antioch and Byzantium and Athens and Rome could be held by the voice of a leader of slaves?

Nay, the Nazarene was not with the servant against his master; neither was He with the master against his servant. He was with no man against another man. He was a man above men, and the streams that ran in His sinews sang together with passion and with might.

If nobility lies in being protective, He was the noblest of all men. If freedom is in thought and word and action, He was the freest of all men. If high birth is in pride that yields only to love and in aloofness that is ever gentle and gracious, then He was of all men the highest born.

Forget not that only the strong and the swift shall win the race and the laurels, and that Jesus was crowned by those who loved Him, and also by His enemies though they knew it not.

Even now He is crowned every day by the priestesses of Artemis in the secret places of her temple.

MATTHEW

UPON AN EVENING JESUS PASSED BY A PRISON THAT WAS in the Tower of David. And we were walking after Him.

Of a sudden He tarried and laid His cheek against the stones of the prison wall. And thus He spoke:

"Brothers of my ancient day, my heart beats with your hearts behind the bars. Would that you could be free in my freedom and walk with me and my comrades.

"You are confined, but not alone. Many are the prisoners who walk the open streets. Their wings are not shorn, but like the peacock they flutter yet cannot fly.

"Brothers of my second day, I shall soon visit you in your cells and yield my shoulder to your burden. For the innocent and the guilty are not parted, and like the two bones of the forearm they shall never be cleaved.

"Brothers of this day, which is my day, you swam against the current of their reasoning and you were caught. They say I too swim against that current. Perhaps I shall soon be with you, a law-breaker among law-breakers.

"Brothers of a day not yet come, these walls shall fall down, and out of the stones other shapes shall be fashioned by Him whose mallet is light, and whose chisel is the wind, and you shall stand free in the freedom of my new day."

Thus spoke Jesus and He walked on, and His hand was upon the prison wall until He passed by the Tower of David.

ANDREW

THE BITTERNESS OF DEATH IS LESS BITTER THAN LIFE without Him. The days were hushed and made still when He was silenced. Only the echo in my memory repeats His words. But not His voice.

Once I heard Him say: "Go forth in your longing to the fields, and sit by the lilies, and you shall hear them humming in the sun. They weave not cloth for raiment, nor do they raise wood or stone for shelter; yet they sing.

"He who works in the night fulfils their needs and the dew of His grace is upon their petals.

"And are not you also His care who never wearies nor rests?"

And once I heard Him say, "The birds of the sky are counted and enrolled by your Father even as the hairs of your head are numbered. Not a bird shall lie at the archer's feet, neither shall a hair of your head turn gray or fall into the emptiness of age without His will."

And once again He said, "I have heard you murmur in your hearts: 'Our God shall be more merciful unto us, children of Abraham, than unto those who knew Him not in the beginning.'

"But I say unto you that the owner of the vineyard who calls a labourer in the morning to reap, and calls another at sundown, and yet renders wages to the last even as to the first, that man is indeed justified. Does he not pay out of his own purse and with his own will?

"So shall my Father open the gate of His mansion at the knocking of the Gentiles even as at your knocking. For His ear heeds the new melody with the same love that it feels for the oft-heard song. And with a special welcome because it is the youngest string of His heart."

And once again I heard Him say, "Remember this: a thief is a man in need, a liar is a man in fear; the hunter who is hunted by the watchman of your night is also hunted by the watchman of his own darkness.

"I would have you pity them all.

"Should they seek your house, see that you open your door and bid them sit at your board. If you do not accept them you shall not be free from whatever they have committed."

And on a day I followed Him to the marketplace of Jerusalem as the others followed Him. And He told us the parable of the prodigal son, and the parable of the merchant who sold all his possessions that he might buy a pearl.

But as He was speaking the Pharisees brought into the midst of the crowd a woman whom they called a harlot. And they confronted Jesus and said to Him, "She defiled her marriage vow, and she was taken in the act."

And He gazed at her; and He placed His hand upon her forehead and looked deep into her eyes.

Then He turned to the men who had brought her to Him, and He looked long at them; and He leaned down and with His finger He began to write upon the earth.

He wrote the name of every man, and beside the name He wrote the sin that every man had committed.

And as He wrote they escaped in shame into the streets.

And ere He had finished writing only that woman and ourselves stood before Him.

And again He looked into her eyes, and He said, "You have loved overmuch. They who brought you here loved but little. But they brought you as a snare for my ensnaring.

"And now go in peace.

"None of them is here to judge you. And if it is in your desire to be wise even as you are loving, then seek me; for the Son of Man will not judge you."

And I wondered then whether He said this to her because He Himself was not without sin.

But since that day I have pondered long, and I know now that only the pure of heart forgive the thirst that leads to dead waters.

And only the sure of foot can give a hand to him who stumbles.

And again and yet again I say, the bitterness of death is less bitter than life without Him.

A RICH MAN

HE SPOKE ILL OF RICH MEN. AND UPON A DAY I QUESTIONED Him saying, "Sir, what shall I do to attain the peace of the spirit?"

And He bade me give my possessions to the poor and follow Him.

But He possessed nothing; therefore He knew not the assurance and the freedom of possessions, nor the dignity and the self-respect that lie within.

In my household there are seven score slaves and stewards; some labor in my groves and vineyards, and some direct my ships to distant isles.

Now had I heeded Him and given my possessions to the poor, what would have befallen my slaves and my servants and their wives and children? They too would have become beggars at the gate of the city or the portico of the temple.

Nay that good man did not fathom the secret of possessions. Because He and His followers lived on the bounty of others He thought all men should live likewise.

Behold a contradiction and a riddle: Should rich men bestow their riches upon the poor, and must the poor have the cup and the loaf of the rich man ere they welcome him to their board?

And must needs the holder of the tower be host to his tenants ere he calls himself lord of his own land?

The ant that stores food for the winter is wiser than a grasshopper that sings one day and hungers another.

Last sabbath one of His followers said in the market-place, "At the threshold of heaven where Jesus may leave His sandals, no other man is worthy to lay his head."

But I ask, at the threshold of whose house that honest vagabond could have left His sandals? He Himself never had a house nor a threshold; and often He went without sandals.

JOHN AT PATMOS

ONCE MORE I WOULD SPEAK OF HIM.

God gave me the voice and the burning lips though not the speech.

And unworthy am I for the fuller word, yet I would summon my heart to my lips.

Jesus loved me and I knew not why.

And I loved Him because He quickened my spirit to heights beyond my stature, and to depths beyond my sounding.

Love is a sacred mystery.

To those who love, it remains forever wordless;

But to those who do not love, it may be but a heartless jest.

Jesus called me and my brother when we were laboring in the field.

I was young then and only the voice of dawn had visited my ears.

But His voice and the trumpet of His voice was the end of my labor and the beginning of my passion.

And there was naught for me then but to walk in the sun and worship the loveliness of the hour.

Could you conceive a majesty too kind to be majestic? And a beauty too radiant to seem beautiful? Could you hear in your dreams a voice shy of its own rapture?

He called me and I followed Him.

That evening I returned to my father's house to get my other cloak.

And I said to my mother, "Jesus of Nazareth would have me in His company."

And she said, "Go His way my son, even like your brother."

And I accompanied Him.

His fragrance called me and commanded me, but only to release me.

Love is a gracious host to his guests though to the unbidden his house is a mirage and a mockery.

Now you would have me explain the miracles of Jesus.

We are all the miraculous gesture of the moment; our Lord and Master was the centre of that moment.

Yet it was not in His desire that His gestures be known.

I have heard Him say to the lame, "Rise and go home, but say not to the priest that I have made you whole."

And Jesus' mind was not with the cripple; it was rather with the strong and the upright. His mind sought and held other minds and His complete spirit visited other spirits.

And in so doing His spirit changed these minds and these spirits.

It seemed miraculous, but with our Lord and Master it was simply like breathing the air of every day.

And now let me speak of other things.

On a day when He and I were alone walking in a field, we were both hungry, and we came to a wild apple tree.

There were only two apples hanging on the bough.

And He held the trunk of the tree with His arm and shook it, and the two apples fell down.

He picked them both up and gave one to me. The other He held in His hand.

In my hunger I ate the apple, and I ate it fast.

Then I looked at Him and I saw that He still held the other apple in His hand.

And He gave it to me saying, "Eat this also."

And I took the apple, and in my shameless hunger I ate it.

And as we walked on I looked upon His face.

But how shall I tell you of what I saw?

A night where candles burn in space,

A dream beyond our reaching;

A noon where all shepherds are at peace and happy that their flocks are grazing;

An eventide, and a stillness, and a home coming;

Then a sleep and a dream.

All these things I saw in His face.

He had given me the two apples. And I knew He was hungry even as I was hungry.

But I now know that in giving them to me He had been satisfied. He Himself ate of other fruit from another tree.

I would tell you more of Him, but how shall I?

When love becomes vast love becomes wordless.

And when memory is overladen it seeks the silent deep.

PETER

ONCE IN CAPERNAUM My LORD AND MASTER SPOKE THUS: "Your neighbour is your other self dwelling behind a wall. In understanding, all walls shall fall down.

"Who knows but that your neighbour is your better self wearing another body? See that you love him as you would love yourself.

"He too is a manifestation of the Most High, whom you do not know.

"Your neighbour is a field where the springs of your hope walk in their green garments, and where the winters of your desire dream of snowy heights.

"Your neighbour is a mirror wherein you shall behold your countenance made beautiful by a joy which you yourself did not know, and by a sorrow you yourself did not share.

"I would have you love your neighbour even as I have loved you."

Then I asked Him saying, "How can I love a neighbour who loves me not, and who covets my property? One who would steal my possessions?"

And He answered, "When you are ploughing and your manservant is sowing the seed behind you, would you stop and look backward and put to flight a sparrow feeding upon a few of your seeds? Should you do this, you were not worthy of the riches of your harvest."

When Jesus had said this, I was ashamed and I was silent. But I was not in fear, for He smiled upon me.

A COBBLER IN JERUSALEM

I LOVED HIM NOT, YET I DID NOT HATE HIM. I listened to Him not to hear His words but rather the sound of His voice; for His voice pleased me.

All that He said was vague to my mind, but the music thereof was clear to my ear.

Indeed were it not for what others have said to me of His teaching, I should not have known even so much as whether He was with Judea or against it.

SUSANNAH OF NAZARETH

A NEIGHBOUR OF MARY

I KNEW MARY THE MOTHER OF JESUS, BEFORE SHE became the wife of Joseph the carpenter, when we were both still unwedded.

In those days Mary would behold visions and hear voices, and she would speak of heavenly ministers who visited her dreams.

And the people of Nazareth were mindful of her, and they observed her going and her coming. And they gazed upon her with kindly eyes, for there were heights in her brows and spaces in her steps.

But some said she was possessed. They said this because she would go only upon her own errands.

I deemed her old while she was young, for there was a harvest in her blossoming and ripe fruit in her spring.

She was born and reared amongst us yet she was like an alien from the North Country. In her eyes there was always the astonishment of one not yet familiar with our faces.

And she was as haughty as Miriam of old who marched with her brothers from the Nile to the wilderness.

Then Mary was betrothed to Joseph the carpenter. When Mary was big with Jesus she would walk among the hills and return at eventide with loveliness and pain in her eyes.

And when Jesus was born I was told that Mary said to her mother, "I am but a tree unpruned. See you to this fruit." Martha the midwife heard her.

After three days I visited her. And there was wonder in her eyes, and her breasts heaved, and her arm was around her first-born like the shell that holds the pearl.

We all loved Mary's babe and we watched Him, for there was a warmth in His being and He throbbed with the pace of His life.

The seasons passed, and He became a boy full of laughter and little wanderings. None of us knew what He would do for He seemed always outside of our race. But He was never rebuked though He was venturous and over-daring.

He played with the other children rather than they with Him.

When He was twelve years old, one day He led a blind man across the brook to the safety of the open road.

And in gratitude the blind man asked Him, Little boy, who are you?"

And He answered, "I am not a little boy. I am Jesus." And the blind man said, "Who is your father?"

And He answered, "God is my Father."

And the blind man laughed and replied, "Well said, my little boy. But who is your mother?"

And Jesus answered, "I am not your little boy. And my mother is the earth."

And the blind man said, "Then behold, I was led by the Son of God and the earth across the stream."

And Jesus answered, "I will lead you wherever you would go, and my eyes will accompany your feet."

And He grew like a precious palm tree in our gardens.

When He was nineteen He was as comely as a hart, and His eyes were like honey and full of the surprise of day.

And upon His mouth there was the thirst of the desert flock for the lake.

He would walk the fields alone and our eyes would follow Him, and the eyes of all the maidens of Nazareth. But we were shy of Him.

Love is forever shy of beauty, yet beauty shall forever be pursued by love.

Then the years bade Him speak in the temple and in the gardens of Galilee. And at times Mary followed Him to listen to His words and to hear the sound of her own heart. But when He and those who loved Him went down to Jerusalem she would not go.

For we of the North Country are often mocked in the streets of Jerusalem, even when we go carrying our offerings to the temple.

And Mary was too proud to yield to the South Country.

And Jesus visited other lands in the east and in the west. We knew not what lands He visited, yet our hearts followed Him.

But Mary awaited Him upon her threshold, and every eventide her eyes sought the road for His home-coming.

Yet upon His return she would say to us, "He is too vast to be my Son, too eloquent for my silent heart. How shall I claim Him?"

It seemed to us that Mary could not believe that the plain had given birth to the mountain; in the whiteness of her heart she did not see that the ridge is a pathway to the summit.

She knew the man, but because He was her Son she dared not know Him.

And on a day when Jesus went to the lake to be with the fishermen she said to me, "What is man but this restless being that would rise from the earth, and who is man but a longing that desires the stars?

"My son is a longing. He is all of us longing for the stars.

"Did I say my son? May God forgive me. Yet in my heart I would be His mother."

Now, it is hard to tell more of Mary and her Son, but though there shall be husks in my throat, and my words shall reach you like cripples on crutches, I must needs relate what I have seen and heard.

It was in the youth of the year when the red anemones were upon the hills that Jesus called His disciples saying to them, "Come with me to Jerusalem and witness the slaying of the lamb for the passover."

Upon that selfsame day Mary came to my door and said, "He is seeking the Holy City. Will you come and follow Him with me and the other women?"

And we walked the long road behind Mary and her son till we reached Jerusalem. And there a company of men and women hailed us at the gate, for His coming had been heralded to those who loved Him.

But upon that very night Jesus left the city with His men. We were told that He had gone to Bethany.

And Mary stayed with us in the inn, awaiting His return.

Upon the eve of the following Thursday He was caught without the walls, and was held prisoner.

And when we heard He was a prisoner, Mary uttered not a word, but there appeared in her eyes the fulfilment of that promised pain and joy which we had beheld when she was but a bride in Nazareth.

She did not weep. She only moved among us like the ghost of a mother who would not bewail the ghost of her son.

We sat low upon the floor but she was erect, walking up and down the room.

She would stand beside the window and gaze eastward, and then with the fingers of her two hands brush back her hair.

At dawn she was still standing among us, like a lone banner in the wilderness wherein there are no hosts.

We wept because we knew the morrow of her son; but she did not weep for she knew also what would befall Him.

Her bones were of bronze and her sinews of the ancient elms, and her eyes were like the sky, wide and daring.

Have you heard a thrush sing while its nest burns in the wind? Have you seen a woman whose sorrow is too much for tears, or a wounded heart that would rise beyond its own pain?

You have not seen such a woman, for you have not stood in the presence of Mary; and you have not been enfolded by the Mother Invisible.

In that still moment when the muffled hoofs of silence beat upon the breasts of the sleepless, John the young son of Zebedee, came and said: "Mary Mother, Jesus is going forth. Come, let us follow Him."

And Mary laid her hand upon John's shoulder and they went out, and we followed them.

When we came to the Tower of David we saw Jesus carrying His cross. And there was a great crowd about Him.

And two other men were also carrying their crosses.

And Mary's head was held high, and she walked with us after her son. And her step was firm.

And behind her walked Zion and Rome, ay, the whole world, to revenge itself upon one free Man.

When we reached the hill, He was raised high upon the cross.

And I looked at Mary. And her face was not the face of a woman bereaved. It was the countenance of the fertile earth, forever giving birth, forever burying her children. Then to her eyes came the remembrance of His childhood, and she said aloud, "My son, who is not my son; man who once visited my womb, I glory in your power. I know that every drop of blood that runs down from your hands shall be the well-stream of a nation.

"You die in this tempest even as my heart once died in the sunset, and I shall not sorrow."

At that moment I desired to cover my face with my cloak and run away to the North Country. But of a sudden I heard Mary say, "My son, who is not my son, what have you said to the man at your right hand that has made him happy in his agony? The shadow of death is light upon his face, and he cannot turn his eyes from you.

"Now you smile upon me, and because you smile I know you have conquered."

And Jesus looked upon His mother and said, "Mary, from this hour be you the mother of John."

And to John He said, "Be a loving son unto this woman. Go to her house and let your shadow cross the threshold where I once stood. Do this in remembrance of me."

And Mary raised her right hand towards Him, and she was like a tree with one branch. And again she cried, "My son, who is not my son, if this be of God may God give us patience and the knowledge thereof. And if it be of man may God forgive him forevermore.

"If it be of God, the snow of Lebanon shall be your shroud; and if it be only of these priests and soldiers, then I have this garment for your nakedness.

"My son, who is not my son, that which God builds here shall not perish; and that which man would destroy shall remain builded, but not in his sight."

And at that moment the heavens yielded Him to the earth, a cry and a breath.

And Mary yielded Him also unto man, a wound and a balsam.

And Mary said, "Now behold, He is gone. The battle is over. The star has shone forth. The ship has reached the harbour. He who once lay against my heart is throbbing in space."

And we came close to her, and she said to us, "Even in death He smiles. He has conquered. I would indeed be the mother of a conqueror."

And Mary returned to Jerusalem leaning upon John the young disciple.

And she was a woman fulfilled.

And when we reached the gate of the city, I gazed upon her face and I was astonished, for on that day the head of Jesus was the highest among men, yet Mary's head was not less high. All this came to pass in the spring of the year.

And now it is autumn. And Mary the mother of Jesus has come again to her dwelling-place, and she is alone.

Two sabbaths ago my heart was as a stone in my breast, for my son had left me for a ship in Tyre. He would be a sailor.

And he said he would return no more.

And upon an evening I sought Mary.

When I entered her house she was sitting at her loom, but she was not weaving. She was looking into the sky beyond Nazareth.

And I said to her, "Hail, Mary."

And she stretched out her arm to me, and said,

Come and sit beside me, and let us watch the sun pour its blood upon the hills."

And I sat beside her on the bench and we gazed into the west through the window.

And after a moment Mary said, "I wonder who is crucifying the sun this eventide."

Then I said, "I came to you for comfort. My son has left me for the sea and I am alone in the house across the way."

Then Mary said, "I would comfort you but how shall I?"

And I said, "If you will only speak of your son I shall be comforted." And Mary smiled upon me, and she laid her hand about my shoulder and she said, "I will speak of Him. That which will console you will give me consolation."

Then she spoke of Jesus, and she spoke long of all that was in the beginning.

And it seemed to me that in her speech she would have no difference between her son and mine.

For she said to me, "My son is also a seafarer. Why would you not trust your son to the waves even as I have trusted Him?

"Woman shall be forever the womb and the cradle but never the tomb. We die that we may give life unto life even as our fingers spin the thread for the raiment that we shall never wear.

"And we cast the net for the fish that we shall never taste.

"And for this we sorrow, yet in all this is our joy."

Thus spoke Mary to me.

And I left her and came to my house, and though the light of the day was spent I sat at my loom to weave more of the cloth.

JOSEPH SURNAMED JUSTUS

THEY SAY HE WAS VULGAR, THE COMMON off spring of common seed, a man uncouth and violent.

They say that only the wind combed His hair, and only the rain brought His clothes and His body together.

They deem Him mad, and they attribute His words to demons.

Yet behold, the Man despised sounded a challenge and the sound thereof shall never cease.

He sang a song and none shall arrest that melody. It shall hover from generation to generation and it shall rise from sphere to sphere remembering the lips that gave it birth and the ears that cradled it.

He was a stranger. Aye, He was a stranger, a wayfarer on His way to a shrine, a visitor who knocked at our door, a guest from a far country.

And because He found not a gracious host, He has returned to His own place.

PHILIP

WHEN OUR BELOVED DIED, ALL MANKIND DIED AND all things for a space were still and gray. Then the east was darkened, and a tempest rushed out of it and swept the land. The eyes of the sky opened and shut, and the rain came down in torrents and carried away the blood that streamed from His hands and His feet.

I too died. But in the depth of my oblivion I heard Him speak and say, "Father forgive them, for they know not what they do."

And His voice sought my drowned spirit and I was brought back to the shore.

And I opened my eyes and I saw His white body hanging against the cloud, and His words that I had heard took shape within me and became a new man. And I sorrowed no more.

Who would sorrow for a sea that is unveiling its face, or for a mountain that laughs in the sun?

Was it ever in the heart of man, when that heart was pierced, to say such words?

What other judge of men has released His judges? And did ever love challenge hate with power more certain of itself?

Was ever such a trumpet beard 'twixt heaven and earth?

Was it known before that the murdered had compassion on his murderers? Or that the meteor stayed his footsteps for the mole?

The seasons shall tire and the years grow old, ere they exhaust these words: "FATHER FORGIVE THEM, FOR THEY KNOW NOT WHAT THEY DO."

And you and I, though born again and again, shall keep them.

And now I would go into my house, and stand an exalted beggar, at His door.

BIRBARAH OF YAMMOUNI

JESUS WAS PATIENT WITH THE DULLARD AND THE stupid, even as the winter awaits the spring.

He was patient like a mountain in the wind. He answered with kindliness the harsh questionings of His foes.

He could even be silent to cavil and dispute, for He was strong and the strong can be forbearing.

But Jesus was also impatient.

He spared not the hypocrite.

He yielded not to men of cunning nor to the jugglers of words.

And He would not be governed.

He was impatient with those who believed not in light because they themselves dwelt in shadow; and with those who sought after signs in the sky rather than in their own hearts.

He was impatient with those who weighed and measured the day and the night before they would trust their dreams to dawn or eventide.

Jesus was patient.

Yet He was the most impatient of men.

He would have you weave the cloth though you spend years between the loom and the linen.

But He would have none tear an inch off the woven fabric.

PILATE'S WIFE TO A ROMAN LADY

I WAS WALKING WITH MY MAIDENS IN THE GROVES outside of Jerusalem when I saw Him with a few men and women sitting about Him; and He was speaking to them in a language which I only half understood.

But one needs not a language to perceive a pillar of light or a mountain of crystal. The heart knows what the tongue may never utter and the ears may never hear.

He was speaking to His friends of love and strength. I know He spoke of love because there was melody in His voice; and I know He spoke of strength because there were armies in His gestures. And He was tender, though even my husband could not have spoken with such authority.

When He saw me passing by He stopped speaking for a moment and looked kindly upon me. And I was humbled; and in my soul I knew I had passed by a god.

After that day His image visited my privacy when I would not be visited by man or woman; and His eyes searched my soul when my own eyes were closed. And His voice governs the stillness of my nights.

I am held fast forevermore; and there is peace in my pain, and freedom in my tears.

Beloved friend, you have never seen that man, and you will never see Him.

He is gone beyond our senses, but of all men He is now the nearest to me.

A MAN OUTSIDE OF JERUSALEM

OF JUDAS

JUDAS CAME TO MY HOUSE THAT FRIDAY, UPON THE EVE of the passover; and he knocked at my door with force.

When he entered I looked at him, and his face was ashen. His hands trembled like dry twigs in the wind, and his clothes were as wet as if he had stepped out from a river; for on that evening there were great tempests.

He looked at me, and the sockets of his eyes were like dark caves and his eyes were blood-sodden.

And he said, "I have delivered Jesus of Nazareth to His enemies and to my enemies."

Then Judas wrung his hands and he said, "Jesus declared that He would overcome all His foes and the foes of our people. And I believed and I followed Him.

"When first He called us to Him He promised us a kingdom mighty and vast, and in our faith we sought His favor that we might have honorable stations in His court.

"We beheld ourselves princes dealing with these Romans as they have dealt with us. And Jesus said much about His kingdom, and I thought He had chosen me a captain of His chariots, and a chief man of His warriors. And I followed His footsteps willingly.

"But I found it was not a kingdom that Jesus sought, nor was it from the Romans He would have had us free. His kingdom was but the kingdom of the heart. I heard Him talk of love and charity and forgiveness, and the wayside women listened gladly, but my heart grew bitter and I was hardened.

"My promised king of Judea seemed suddenly to have turned flute-player, to soothe the mind of wanderers and vagabonds.

"I had loved Him as others of my tribe had loved Him. I had beheld in Him a hope and a deliverance from the yoke of the aliens. But when He would not utter a word or move a hand to free us from that yoke, and when He would even have rendered unto Caesar that which is Caesar's, then despair filled me and my hopes died. And I said, 'He who murders my hopes shall be murdered, for my hopes and expectations are more precious than the life of any man.'"

Then Judas gnashed his teeth; and he bent down his head. And when he spoke again, he said, "I have delivered Him up. And He was crucified this day.... Yet when He died upon the cross, He died a king. He died in the tempest as deliverers die, like vast men who live beyond the shroud and the stone.

"And all the while He was dying, He was gracious, and He was kindly; and His heart was full of pity. He felt pity even for me who had delivered Him up."

And I said, "Judas, you have committed a grave wrong."

And Judas answered, "But He died a king. Why did He not live a king?"

And I said again, "You have committed a grave crime."

And he sat down there, upon that bench, and he was as still as a stone.

But I walked to and fro in the room, and once more I said, "You have committed a great sin."

But Judas said not a word. He remained as silent as the earth.

And after a while he stood up and faced me and he seemed taller, and when he spoke his voice was like the sound of a cracked vessel; and he said, "Sin was not in my heart. This very night I shall seek His kingdom, and I shall stand in His presence and beg His forgiveness.

"He died a king, and I shall die a felon. But in my heart I know He will forgive me."

After saying these words he folded his wet cloak around him and he said, " It was good that I came to you this night even though I have brought you trouble. Will you also forgive me?

"Say to your sons and to your sons' sons: 'Judas Iscariot delivered Jesus of Nazareth to His enemies because he believed Jesus was an enemy to His own race.'

"And say also that Judas upon the selfsame day of his great error followed the King to the steps of His throne to deliver up his own soul and to be judged.

"I shall tell Him that my blood also was impatient for the sod, and my crippled spirit would be free."

Then Judas leaned his head back against the wall and he cried out, "O God whose dreaded name no man shall utter ere his lips are touched by the fingers of death, why did you burn me with a fire that had no light?

"Why did you give the Galilean a passion for a land unknown and burden me with desire that would not escape kin or hearth? And who is this man Judas, whose hands are dipped in blood?

"Lend me a hand to cast him off, an old garment and a tattered harness.

"Help me to do this tonight.

"And let me stand again outside of these walls.

"I am weary of this wingless liberty. I would a larger dungeon.

"I would flow a stream of tears to the bitter sea. I would be a man of your mercy rather than one knocking at the gate of his own heart."

Thus Judas spoke, and thereupon he opened the door and went out again into the tempest. Three days afterwards I visited Jerusalem and heard of all that had come to pass. And I also heard that Judas had flung himself from the summit of the High Rock.

I have pondered long since that day, and I understand Judas. He fulfilled his little life, which hovered like a mist on this land enslaved by the Romans, while the great prophet was ascending the heights.

One man longed for a kingdom in which he was to be a prince.

Another man desired a kingdom in which all men shall be princes.

SARKIS

AN OLD GREEK SHEPHERD

CALLED THE MADMAN

IN A DREAM I SAW JESUS AND MY GOD PAN SITTING together in the heart of the forest.

They laughed at each other's speech, with the brook that ran near them, and the laughter of Jesus was the merrier. And they conversed long.

Pan spoke of earth and her secrets, and of his hoofed brothers and his horned sisters; and of dreams. And he spoke of roots and their nestlings, and of the sap that wakes and rises and sings to summer.

And Jesus told of the young shoots in the forest, and of flowers and fruit, and the seed that they shall bear in a season not yet come.

He spoke of birds in space and their singing in the upper world.

And He told of white harts in the desert wherein God shepherds them.

And Pan was pleased with the speech of the new God, and his nostrils quivered.

And in the same dream I beheld Pan and Jesus grow quiet and still in the stillness of the green shadows.

And then Pan took his reeds and played to Jesus. The trees were shaken and the ferns trembled, and there was a fear upon me.

And Jesus said, "Good brother, you have the glade and the rocky height in your reeds."

Then Pan gave the reeds to Jesus and said, "You play now. It is your turn."

And Jesus said, "These reeds are too many for my mouth. I have this flute."

And He took His flute and He played.

And I heard the sound of rain in the leaves, and the singing of streams among the hills, and the falling of snow on the mountain-top.

The pulse of my heart, that had once beaten with the wind, was restored again to the wind, and all the waves of my yesterdays were upon my shore, and I was again Sarkis the shepherd, and the flute of Jesus became the pipes of countless shepherds calling to countless flocks.

Then Pan said to Jesus, "Your youth is more kin to the reed than my years. And long ere this in my stillness I have heard your song and the murmur of your name.

"Your name has a goodly sound; well shall it rise with the sap to the branches, and well shall it run with the hoofs among the hills.

"And it is not strange to me, though my father called me not by that name. It was your flute that brought it back to my memory.

"And now let us play our reeds together."

And they played together.

And their music smote heaven and earth, and a terror struck all living things.

I heard the bellow of beasts and the hunger of the forest. And I heard the cry of lonely men, and the plaint of those who long for what they know not.

I heard the sighing of the maiden for her lover, and the panting of the luckless hunter for his prey.

And then there came peace into their music, and the heavens and the earth sang together.

All this I saw in my dream, and all this I heard.

ANNAS

THE HIGH PRIEST

HE WAS OF THE RABBLE, A BRIGAND, A MOUNTEBANK and a self-trumpeter. He appealed only to the unclean and the disinherited, and for this He had to go the way of all the tainted and the defiled.

He made sport of us and of our laws; He mocked at our honor and jeered at our dignity. He even said He would destroy the temple and desecrate the holy places. He was shameless, and for this He had to die a shameful death.

He was a man from Galilee of the Gentiles, an alien, from that North Country where Adonis and Ashtarte still claim power against Israel and the God of Israel.

He whose tongue halted when He spoke the speech of our prophets was loud and ear-splitting when He spoke the bastard language of the lowborn and the vulgar.

What else was there for me but to decree His death?

Am I not a guardian of the temple? Am I not a keeper of the law? Could I have turned my back on Him, saying in all tranquillity: "He is a madman among madmen. Let Him alone to exhaust Himself raving; for the mad and the crazed and those possessed with devils shall be naught in the path of Israel"?

Could I have been deaf unto Him when He called us liars, hypocrites, wolves, vipers, and the sons of vipers?

Nay I could not be deaf to Him, for He was not a madman. He was self-possessed; and in His big-sounding sanity He denounced and challenged us all.

For this I had Him crucified, and His crucifixion was a signal and warning unto the others who are stamped with the same damned seal.

I know well I have been blamed for this, even by some of the elders in the Sanhedrim. But I was mindful then as I am mindful now, that one man should die for the people rather than the people be led astray by one man.

Judea was conquered by an enemy from without. I shall see that Judea is not conquered again, by an enemy from within.

No man from the cursed North shall reach our Holy of Holies nor lay His shadow across the Ark of the Covenant.

A WOMAN

ONE OF MARY'S NEIGHBOURS

ON THE FORTIETH DAY AFTER HIS DEATH, ALL THE WOMEN NEIGHBOURS CAME TO THE HOUSE OF MARY TO CONSOLE HER AND TO SING THRENODIES.

And one of the women sang this song:

Whereto my Spring, whereto?
And to what other space your perfume ascending?
In what other fields shall you walk?
And to what sky shall you lift up your head to speak your heart?

These valleys shall be barren,
And we shall have naught but dried fields and arid.
All green things will parch in the sun,
And our orchards will bring forth sour apples,
And our vineyards bitter grapes.
We shall thirst for your wine,
And our nostrils will long for your fragrance.

Whereto Flower of our first spring, whereto?
And will you return no more?
Will not your jasmine visit us again,
And your cyclamen stand by our wayside
To tell us that we too have our roots deep in earth,
And that our ceaseless breath would forever climb the sky.?

Whereto Jesus, whereto, Son of my neighbour Mary,
And comrade to my son?
Whither, our first Spring, and to what other fields?
Will you return to us again?
Will you in your love-tide visit the barren shores of our dreams?

AHAZ THE PORTLY

THE KEEPER OF THE INN

WELL DO I REMEMBER THE LAST TIME I SAW JESUS THE Nazarene. Judas had come to me at the noon hour of that Thursday, and bidden me prepare supper for Jesus and His friends.

He gave me two silver pieces and said, "Buy all that you deem needful for the meal."

And after He was gone my wife said to me,

This is indeed a distinction." For Jesus had become a prophet and He had wrought many miracles.

At twilight He came and His followers, and they sat in the upper chamber around the board, but they were silent and quiet.

Last year also and the year before they had come and then they had been joyous. They broke the bread and drank the wine and sang our ancient strains; and Jesus would talk to them till midnight.

After that they would leave Him alone in the upper chamber and go to sleep in other rooms; for after midnight it was His desire to be alone.

And He would remain awake; I would hear His steps as I lay upon my bed.

But this last time He and His friends were not happy. My wife had prepared fishes from the Lake of Galilee, and pheasants from Houran stuffed with rice and pomegranate seeds, and I had carried them a jug of my cypress wine.

And then I had left them for I felt that they wished to be alone.

They stayed until it was full dark, and then they all descended together from the upper chamber, but at the foot of the stairs Jesus tarried awhile. And He looked at me and my wife, and He placed His hand upon the head of my daughter and He said, "Good night to you all. We shall come back again to your upper chamber, but we shall not leave you at this early hour. We shall stay until the sun rises above the horizon.

"In a little while we shall return and ask for more bread and more wine. You and your wife have been good hosts to us, and we shall remember you when we come to our mansion and sit at our own board."

And I said, "Sir, it was an honor to serve you. The other innkeepers envy me because of your visits, and in my pride I smile at them in the marketplace. Sometimes I even make a grimace."

And He said, "All innkeepers should be proud in serving. For he who gives bread and wine is the brother of him who reaps and gathers the sheaves for the threshing-floor, and of him who crushes the grapes at the winepress. And you are all kindly. You give of your bounty even to those who come with naught but hunger and thirst."

Then He turned to Judas Iscariot who kept the purse of the company, and He said, "Give me two shekels."

And Judas gave Him two shekels saying: "These are the last silver pieces in my purse."

Jesus looked at him and said, "Soon, oversoon, your purse shall be filled with silver."

Then He put the two pieces into my hand and said, "With these buy a silken girdle for your daughter, and bid her wear it on the day of the passover in remembrance of me."

And looking again into the face of my daughter, He leaned down and kissed her brow. And then He said once more, "Good-night to you all."

And He walked away.

I have been told that what He said to us has been recorded upon a parchment by one of His friends, but I repeat it to you even as I heard it from His own lips.

Never shall I forget the sound of His voice as He said those words, "Good night to you all."

If you would know more of Him, ask my daughter. She is a woman now, but she cherishes the memory of her girlhood. And her words are more ready than mine.

BARABBAS

THE LAST WORDS OF JESUS

THEY RELEASED ME AND CHOSE HIM. THEN HE ROSE and I fell down.

And they held Him a victim and a sacrifice for the passover.

I was freed from my chains, and walked with the throng behind Him, but I was a living man going to my own grave.

I should have fled to the desert where shame is burned out by the sun.

Yet I walked with those who had chosen Him to bear my crime.

When they nailed Him on His cross I stood there.

I saw and I heard but I seemed outside of my body.

The thief who was crucified on His right said to Him, "Are you bleeding with me, even you, Jesus of Nazareth?"

And Jesus answered and said, "Were it not for this nail that stays my hand I would reach forth and clasp your hand.

"We are crucified together. Would they had raised your cross nearer to mine."

Then He looked down and gazed upon His mother and a young man who stood

beside her.

He said, "Mother, behold your son standing beside you.

"Woman, behold a man who shall carry these drops of my blood to the North Country."

And when He heard the wailing of the women of Galilee He said: "Behold, they weep and I thirst.

"I am held too high to reach their tears.

"I will not take vinegar and gall to quench this thirst."

Then His eyes opened wide to the sky, and He said: "Father, why hast Thou forsaken us?"

And then He said in compassion, "Father, forgive them, for they know not what they do."

When He uttered these words me thought I saw all men prostrated before God beseeching forgiveness for the crucifixion of this one man.

Then again He said with a great voice "Father, into Thy hand I yield back my spirit."

And at last He lifted up His head and said, "Now it is finished, but only upon this hill."

And He closed His eyes.

Then lightning cracked the dark skies, and there was a great thunder.

I know now that those who slew Him in my stead achieved my endless torment.

His crucifixion endured but for an hour.

But I shall be crucified unto the end of my years.

CLAUDIUS

A ROMAN SENTINEL

AFTER HE WAS TAKEN, THEY ENTRUSTED HIM TO ME. And I was ordered by Pontius Pilatus to keep Him in custody until the following morning.

My soldiers led Him prisoner, and He was obedient to them.

At midnight I left my wife and children and visited the arsenal. It was my habit to go about and see that all was well with my battalions in Jerusalem; and that night I visited the arsenal where He was held.

My soldiers and some of the young Jews were making sport of Him. They had stripped Him of His garment, and they had put a crown of last year's brier-thorns upon His head.

They had seated Him against a pillar, and they were dancing and shouting before Him.

And they had given Him a reed to hold in His hand.

As I entered someone shouted: "Behold, O Captain, the King of the Jews."

I stood before Him and looked at Him, and I was ashamed. I knew not why.

I had fought in Gallia and in pain, an with my men I had faced death. Yet never had I been in fear, nor been a coward. But when I stood before that man and He looked at me I lost heart. It seemed as though my lips were sealed, and I could utter no word.

And straightway I left the arsenal.

This chanced thirty years ago. My sons who were babes then are men now. And they are serving Caesar and Rome.

But often in counselling them I have spoken of Him, a man facing death with the sap of life upon His lips, and with compassion for His slayers in His eyes.

And now I am old. I have lived the years fully. And I think truly that neither Pompey nor Caesar was so great a commander as that Man of Galilee.

For since His unresisting death an army has risen out of the earth to fight for Him.... And He is better served by them, though dead, than ever Pompey or Caesar was served, though living.

JAMES THE BROTHER OF

THE LORD

THE LAST SUPPER

A THOUSAND TIMES I HAVE BEEN VISITED BY THE MEMORY of that night. And I know now that I shall be visited a thousand times again.

The earth shall forget the furrows ploughed upon her breast, and a woman the pain and joy of childbirth, ere I shall forget that night.

In the afternoon we had been outside the walls of Jerusalem, and Jesus had said, "Let us go into the city now and take supper at the inn."

It was dark when we reached the inn, and we were hungry. The innkeeper greeted us and led us to an upper chamber.

And Jesus bade us sit around the board, but He Himself remained standing, and His eyes rested upon us.

And He spoke to the keeper of the inn and said, "Bring me a basin and a pitcher full of water, and a towel."

And He looked at us again and said gently, Cast off your sandals."

We did not understand, but at His command we cast them off.

Then the keeper of the inn brought the basin and the pitcher; and Jesus said, "Now I will wash your feet. For I must needs free your feet from the dust of the ancient road, and give them the freedom of the new way."

And we were all abashed and shy.

Then Simon Peter stood up and said: "How shall I suffer my Master and my Lord to wash my feet?"

And Jesus answered, "I will wash your feet that you may remember that he who serves men shall be the greatest among men."

Then He looked at each one of us and He said:

The Son of Man who has chosen you for His brethren, He whose feet were anointed yesterday with myrrh of Arabia and dried with a woman's hair, desires now to wash your feet."

And He took the basin and the pitcher and kneeled down and washed our feet, beginning with Judas Iscariot.

Then He sat down with us at the board; and His face was like the dawn rising upon a battlefield after a night of strife and blood-shedding.

And the keeper of the inn came with his wife, bringing food and wine.

And though I had been hungry before Jesus knelt at my feet, now I had no stomach for food. And there was a flame in my throat which I would not quench with wine.

Then Jesus took a loaf of bread and gave to us, saying, "Perhaps we shall not break bread again. Let us eat this morsel in remembrance of our days in Galilee."

And He poured wine from the jug into a cup, and He drank, and gave to us, and He said, "Drink this in remembrance of a thirst we have known together. And drink it also in hope for the new vintage. When I am enfolded and am no more among you, and when you meet here or elsewhere, break the bread and pour the wine, and eat and drink even as you are doing now. Then look about you; and perchance you may see me sitting with you at the board."

After saying this He began to distribute among us morsels of fish and pheasant, like a bird feeding its fledglings.

We ate little yet we were filled; and we drank but a drop, for we felt that the cup was like a space between this land and another land.

Then Jesus said, "Ere we leave this board let us rise and sing the joyous hymns of Galilee."

And we rose and sang together, and His voice was above our voices, and there was a ringing in every word of His words.

And He looked at our faces, each and every one, and He said, "Now I bid you farewell. Let us go beyond these walls. Let us go unto Gethsemane."

And John the son of Zebedee said, "Master, why do you say farewell to us this night?"

And Jesus said, "Let not your heart be troubled. I only leave you to prepare a place for you in my Father's house. But if you shall be in need of me, I will come back to you. Where you call me, there I shall hear you, and wherever your spirit shall seek me, there I will be.

"Forget not that thirst leads to the winepress, and hunger to the wedding-feast.

"It is in your longing that you shall find the Son of Man. For longing is the fountain-head of ecstasy, and it is the path to the Father."

And John spoke again and said, "If you would indeed leave us, how shall we be of good cheer? And why speak you of separation?"

And Jesus said, "The hunted stag knows the arrow of the hunter before he feels it in his breast; and the river is aware of the sea ere it comes to her shore. And the Son of Man has travelled the ways of men.

"Before another almond tree renders her blossoms to the sun, my roots shall be reaching into the heart of another field."

Then Simon Peter said: "Master, leave us not now, and deny us not the joy of your presence. Where you go we too will go; and wherever you abide there we will be also."

And Jesus put His hand upon Simon Peter's shoulder, and smiled upon him, and He said, "Who knows but that you may deny me before this night is over, and leave me before I leave you?"

Then of a sudden He said, "Now let us go hence."

And He left the inn and we followed Him. But when we reached the gate of the city, Judas of Iscariot was no longer with us. And we crossed the Valley of Jahannam. Jesus walked far ahead of us, and we walked close to one another.

When He reached an, olive grove He stopped and turned towards us saying, "Rest here for an hour."

The evening was cool, though it was full spring with the mulberries unfolding their shoots and the apple trees in bloom. And the gardens were sweet.

Each one of us sought the trunk of a tree, and we lay down. I myself gathered my cloak around me and lay under a pine tree.

But Jesus left us and walked by Himself in the olive grove. And I watched Him while the others slept.

He would suddenly stand still, and again He would walk up and down. This He did many times.

Then I saw Him lift His face towards the sky and outstretch His arms to cast and west.

Once He had said, "Heaven and earth, and hell too, are of man." And now I remembered His saying, and I knew that He who was pacing the olive grove was heaven made man; and I bethought me that the womb of the earth is not a beginning nor an end, but rather a chariot, a pause; and a moment of wonder and surprise; and hell I saw also, in the valley called Jahannam, which lay between Him and the Holy City.

And as He stood there and I lay wrapped in my garment, I heard His voice speaking. But He was not speaking to us. Thrice I heard Him pronounce the word FATHER. And that was all I heard.

After a while His arms dropped down, and He stood still like a cypress tree between my eyes and the sky.

At last He came over among us again, and He said to us, "Wake and rise. My hour has come. The world is already upon us, armed for battle."

And then He said, "A moment ago I heard the voice of my Father. If I see you not again, remember that the conqueror shall not have peace until he is conquered."

And when we had risen and come close to Him, His face was like the starry heaven above the desert.

Then He kissed each one of us upon the cheek. And when His lips touched my cheek, they were hot, like the hand of a child in fever.

Suddenly we heard a great noise in the distance, as of numbers, and when it came near it was a company of men approaching with lanterns and staves. And they came in haste.

As they reached the hedge of the grove Jesus left us and went forth to meet them. And Judas of Iscariot was leading them.

There were Roman soldiers with swords and spears, and men of Jerusalem with clubs and pickaxes.

And Judas came up to Jesus and kissed Him. And then he said to the armed men, "This is the Man."

And Jesus said to Judas, "Judas, you were patient with me. This could have been yesterday."

Then He turned to the armed men and said: "Take me now. But see that your cage is large enough for these wings."

Then they fell upon Him and held Him, and they were all shouting.

But we in our fear ran away and sought to escape. I ran alone through the olive groves, nor had I power to be mindful, nor did any voice speak in me except my fear.

Through the two or three hours that remained of that night I was fleeing and hiding, and at dawn I found myself in a village near Jericho.

Why had I left Him? I do not know. But to my sorrow I did leave Him. I was a coward and I fled from the face of His enemies.

Then I was sick and ashamed at heart, and I returned to Jerusalem, but He was a prisoner, and no friend could have speech with Him.

He was crucified, and His blood has made new clay of the earth.

And I am living still; I am living upon the honeycomb of His sweet life.

SIMON THE CYRENE

I WAS ON MY WAY TO THE FIELDS WHEN I SAW Him carrying His cross; and multitudes were following Him.

Then I too walked beside Him.

His burden stopped Him many a time, for His body was exhausted.

Then a Roman soldier approached me, saying,

Come, you are strong and firm built; carry the cross of this man."

When I heard these words my heart swelled within me and I was grateful.

And I carried His cross.

It was heavy, for it was made of poplar soaked through with the rains of winter.

And Jesus looked at me. And the sweat of His forehead was running down upon His beard.

Again He looked at me and He said, "Do you too drink this cup? You shall indeed sip its rim with me to the end of time."

So saying He placed His hand upon my free shoulder. And we walked together towards the Hill of the Skull.

But now I felt not the weight of the cross. I felt only His hand. And it was like the wing of a bird upon my shoulder. Then we reached the hill top, and there they were to crucify Him.

And then I felt the weight of the tree.

He uttered no word when they drove the nails into His hands and feet, nor made He any sound.

And His limbs did not quiver under the hammer.

It seemed as if His hands and feet had died and would only live again when bathed in blood. Yet it seemed also as if He sought the nails as the prince would seek the sceptre; and that He craved to be raised to the heights.

And my heart did not think to pity Him, for I was too filled with wonder.

Now, the man whose cross I carried has become my cross.

Should they say to me again, "Carry the cross of this man," I would carry it till my road ended at the grave.

But I would beg Him to place His hand upon my shoulder.

This happened many years ago; and still whenever I follow the furrow in the field, and in that drowsy moment before sleep, I think always of that. Beloved Man.

And I feel His winged hand, here, on my left shoulder.

CYBOREA

THE MOTHER OF JUDAS

MY SON WAS A GOOD MAN AND UPRIGHT. HE WAS TENDER and kind to me, and he loved his kin and his countrymen. And he hated our enemies, the cursed Romans, who wear purple cloth though they spin no thread nor sit at any loom; and who reap and gather where they have not ploughed nor sowed the seed.

My son was but seventeen when he was caught shooting arrows at the Roman legion passing through our vineyard.

Even at that age he would speak to the other youths of the glory of Israel, and he would utter many strange things that I did not understand.

He was my son, my only son.

He drank life from these breasts now dry, and he took his first steps in this garden, grasping these fingers that are now like trembling reeds.

With these selfsame hands, young and fresh then like the grapes of Lebanon, I put away his first sandals in a linen kerchief that my mother had given me. I still keep them there in that chest, beside the window.

He was my first-born, and when he took his first step, I too took my first step. For women travel not save when led by their children. And now they tell me he is dead by his own hand; that he flung himself from the High Rock in remorse because he had betrayed his friend Jesus of Nazareth.

I know my son is dead. But I know he betrayed no one; for he loved his kin and hated none but the Romans.

My son sought the glory of Israel, and naught but that glory was upon his lips and in his deeds.

When he met Jesus on the highway he left me to follow Him. And in my heart I knew that he was wrong to follow any man.

When he bade me farewell I told him that he was wrong, but he listened not.

Our children do not heed us; like the high tide of today, they take no counsel with the high tide of yesterday.

I beg you question me no further about my son.

I loved him and I shall love him forevermore.

If love were in the flesh I would burn it out with hot irons and be at peace. But it is in the soul, unreachable.

And now I would speak no more. Go question another woman more honored than the mother of Judas.

Go to the mother of Jesus. The sword is in her heart also; she will tell you of me, and you will understand.

THE WOMAN OF BYBLOS

A LAMENTATION

WEEP WITH ME, YE DAUGHTERS OF ASH TARTE, and all ye lovers of Tamouz.

Bid your heart melt and rise and run blood-tears,
For He who was made of gold and ivory is no more.
In the dark forest the boar overcame Him,
And the tusks of the boar pierced His flesh.
Now He lies stained with the leaves of yesteryear,
And no longer shall His footsteps wake the seeds that sleep in the bosom of spring.
His voice will not come with the dawn to my window,
And I shall be forever alone.

Weep with me, ye daughters of Ashtarte, and all ye lovers of Tamouz,
For my Beloved has escaped me;
He who spoke as the rivers speak;
He whose voice and time were twins;
He whose mouth was a red pain made sweet;
He on whose lips gall would turn to honey.

Weep with me, daughters of Ashtarte, and ye lovers of Tamouz.
Weep with me around His bier as the stars weep,
And as the moon-petals fall upon His wounded body.
Wet with your tears the silken covers of my bed,
Where my Beloved once lay in my dream,
And was gone away in my awakening.

I charge ye, daughters of Ashtarte, and all ye lovers of Tamouz,
Bare your breasts and weep and comfort me,
For Jesus of Nazareth is dead.

MARY MAGDALEN

THIRTY YEARS LATER

ONCE AGAIN I SAY THAT WITH DEATH JESUS CONQUERED death, and rose from the grave a spirit and a power. And He walked in our solitude and visited the gardens of our passion.

He lies not there in that cleft rock behind the stone.

We who love Him beheld Him with these our eyes which He made to see; and we touched Him with these our hands which He taught to reach forth.

I know you who believe not in Him. I was one of you, and you are many; but your number shall be diminished.

Must you break your harp and your lyre to find the music therein?

Or must you fell a tree ere you can believe it bears fruit?

You hate Jesus because someone from the North Country said He was the Son of God. But you hate one another because each of you deems himself too great to be the brother of the next man.

You hate Him because someone said He was born of a virgin, and not of man's seed.

But you know not the mothers who go to the tomb in virginity, nor the men who go down to the grave choked with their own thirst.

You know not that the earth was given in marriage to the sun, and that earth it is who sends us forth to the mountain and the desert.

There is a gulf that yawns between those who love Him and those who hate Him, between those who believe and those who do not believe.

But when the years have bridged that gulf you shall know that He who lived in us is deathless, that He was the Son of God even as we are the children of God; that He was born of a virgin even as we are born of the husbandless earth.

It is passing strange that the earth gives not to the unbelievers the roots that would suck at her breast, nor the wings wherewith to fly high and drink, and be filled with the dews of her space.

But I know what I know, and it is enough.

A MAN FROM LEBANON

NINETEEN CENTURIES AFTERWARD

MASTER, MASTER SINGER,
Master of words unspoken,
Seven times was I born, and seven times have I died
Since your hasty visit and our brief welcome.
And behold I live again,
Remembering a day and a night among the hills,
When your tide lifted us up.
Thereafter many lands and many seas did I cross,
And wherever I was led by saddle or sail
Your name was prayer or argument.
Men would bless you or curse you;
The curse, a protest against failure,
The blessing, a hymn of the hunter
Who comes back from the hills
With provision for his mate.

—

Your friends are yet with us for comfort and support,
And your enemies also, for strength and assurance.
Your mother is with us;
I have beheld the sheen of her face in the countenance of all mothers;
Her hand rocks cradles with gentleness,
Her hand folds shrouds with tenderness.
And Mary Magdalen is yet in our midst,
She who drank the vinegar of life, and then its wine.
And Judas, the man of pain and small ambitions,
He too walks the earth;
Even now he preys upon himself when his hunger finds naught else,
And seeks his larger self in self-destruction.

—

And John, he whose youth loved beauty, is here,
And he sings though unheeded.
And Simon Peter the impetuous, who denied you that he might live longer for you,
He too sits by our fire.
He may deny you again ere the dawn of another day,
Yet he would be crucified for your purpose, and deem himself unworthy of the honor.
And Caiaphas and Annas still live their day,
And judge the guilty and the innocent.
They sleep upon their feathered bed
Whilst he whom they have judged is whipped with the rods.

—

And the woman who was taken in adultery,
She too walks the streets of our cities,
And hungers for bread not yet baked,
And she is alone in an empty house.
And Pontius Pilatus is here also:
He stands in awe before you,
And still questions you,
But he dares not risk his station or defy an alien race;
And he is still washing his hands.
Even now Jerusalem holds the basin and Rome the ewer,
And betwixt the two a thousand thousand hands would be washed to whiteness.

—

Master, Master Poet,
Master of words sung and spoken,
They have builded temples to house your name,
And upon every height they have raised your cross,
A sign and a symbol to guide their wayward feet,
But not unto your joy.
Your joy is a hill beyond their vision,
And it does not comfort them.
They would honor the man unknown to them.
And what consolation is there in a man like themselves, a man whose kindliness is like their own kindliness,
A god whose love is like their own love,
And whose mercy is in their own mercy?
They honor not the man, the living man,
The first man who opened His eyes and gazed at the sun
With eyelids unquivering.
Nay, they do not know Him, and they would not be like Him.

They would be unknown, walking in the procession of the unknown.
They would bear sorrow, their sorrow,
And they would not find comfort in your joy.
Their aching heart seeks not consolation in your words and the song thereof.
And their pain, silent and unshapen,
Makes them creatures lonely and unvisited.
Though hemmed about by kin and kind,
They live in fear, uncomraded;
Yet they would not be alone.
They would bend eastward when the west wind blows.

They call you king,
And they would be in your court.
They pronounce you the Messiah,
And they would themselves be anointed with the holy oil.
Yea, they would live upon your life.
—
Master, Master Singer,
Your tears were like the showers of May,
And your laughter like the waves of the white sea.
When you spoke Your words were the far-off whisper
of their lips when those lips should be kindled with fire;
You laughed for the marrow in their bones that was not yet ready for laughter;
And you wept for their eyes that yet were dry.
Your voice fathered their thoughts and their under standing.
Your voice mothered their words and their breath.
—
Seven times was I born and seven times have I died,
And now I live again, and I behold you,
The fighter among fighters,
The poet of poets,
King above all kings,
A man half-naked with your road-fellows.
Every day the bishop bends down his head
When he pronounces your name.
And every day the beggars say:
"For Jesus' sake
Give us a penny to buy bread."
We call upon each other,
But in truth we call upon you,
Like the flood tide in the spring of our want and desire,
And when our autumn comes, like the ebb tide.
High or low, your name is upon our lips,
The Master of infinite compassion.
Master, Master of our lonely hours,
Here and there, betwixt the cradle and the coffin, I meet your silent brothers,
The free men, unshackled,
Sons of your mother earth and space.
They are like the birds of the sky,
And like the lilies of the field.
They live your life and think your thoughts,
And they echo your song.
But they are empty-handed,
And they are not crucified with the great crucifixion.

And therein is their pain.
The world crucifies them every day,
But only in little ways.
The sky is not shaken,
And the earth travails not with her dead.
They are crucified and there is none to witness their agony.
They turn their face to right and left
And find not one to promise them a station in his kingdom.
Yet they would be crucified again and yet again,
That your God may be their God,
And your Father their Father.

—

Master, Master Lover,
The Princess awaits your coming in her fragrant chamber,
And the married unmarried woman in her cage;
The harlot who seeks bread in the streets of her shame,
And the nun in her cloister who has no husband;
The childless woman too at her window,
Where frost designs the forest on the pane,
She finds you in that symmetry,
And she would mother you, and be comforted.

—

Master, Master Poet,
Master of our silent desires,
The heart of the world quivers with the throbbing of your heart,
But it burns not with your song.
The world sits listening to your voice in tranquil delight,
But it rises not from its seat
To scale the ridges of your hills.
Man would dream your dream but he would not wake to your dawn
Which is his greater dream.
He would see with your vision,
But he would not drag his heavy feet to your throne.
Yet many have been enthroned in your name
And mitred with your power,
And have turned your golden visit
Into crowns for their head and sceptres for their hand.
Master, Master of Light,
Whose eye dwells in the seeking fingers of the blind,
You are still despised and mocked,
A man too weak and infirm to be God,
A God too much man to call forth adoration.
Their mass and their hymn,
Their sacrament and their rosary, are for their imprisoned self.
You are their yet distant self, their far-off cry, and their passion.

—

But Master, Sky-heart, Knight of our fairer dream,
You do still tread this day;
Nor bows nor spears shall stay your steps.
You walk through all our arrows.
You smile down upon us,
And though you are the youngest of us all
You father us all.

Poet, Singer, Great Heart,
May our God bless your name,
And the womb that held you, and the breasts that gave you milk.
And may God forgive us all.

THE END

The Wanderer

CONTENTS

THE WANDERER

I met him at the crossroads, a man with but a cloak and a staff, and a veil of pain upon his face. And we greeted one another, and I said to him, "Come to my house and be my guest."

And he came.

My wife and my children met us at the threshold, and he smiled at them, and they loved his coming.

Then we all sat together at the board and we were happy with the man for there was a silence and a mystery in him.

And after supper we gathered to the fire and I asked him about his wanderings.

He told us many a tale that night and also the next day, but what I now record was born out of the bitterness of his days though he himself was kindly, and these tales are of the dust and patience of his road.

And when he left us after three days we did not feel that a guest had departed but rather that one of us was still out in the garden and had not yet come in.

GARMENTS

Upon a day Beauty and Ugliness met on the shore of a sea. And they said to one another, "Let us bathe in the sea."

Then they disrobed and swam in the waters. And after a while Ugliness came back to shore and garmented himself with the garments of Beauty and walked away.

And Beauty too came out of the sea, and found not her raiment, and she was too shy to be naked, therefore she dressed herself with the raiment of Ugliness. And Beauty walked her way.

And to this very day men and women mistake the one for the other.

Yet some there are who have beheld the face of Beauty, and they know her notwithstanding her garments. And some there be who know the face of Ugliness, and the cloth conceals him not from their eyes.

THE EAGLE AND THE SKYLARK

A skylark and an eagle met on a rock upon a high hill. The skylark said, "Good morrow to you, Sir." And the eagle looked down upon him and said faintly, "Good morrow."

And the skylark said, "I hope all things are well with you, Sir."

"Aye," said the eagle, "all is well with us. But do you not know that we are the king of birds, and that you shall not address us before we ourselves have spoken?"

Said the skylark, "Methinks we are of the same family."

The eagle looked upon him with disdain and he said, "Who ever has said that you and I are of the same family?"

Then said the skylark, "But I would remind you of this, I can fly even as high as you, and I can sing and give delight to the other creatures of this earth. And you give neither pleasure nor delight."

Then the eagle was angered, and he said, "Pleasure and delight! You little presumptuous creature! With one thrust of my beak I could destroy you. You are but the size of my foot."

Then the skylark flew up and alighted upon the back of the eagle and began to pick at his feathers. The eagle was annoyed, and he flew swift and high that he might rid himself of the little bird. But he failed to do so. At last he dropped back to that very rock upon the high hill, more fretted than ever, with the little creature still upon his back, and cursing the fate of the hour.

Now at that moment a small turtle came by and laughed at the sight, and laughed so hard the she almost turned upon her back.

And the eagle looked down upon the turtle and he said, "You slow creeping thing, ever one with the earth, what are you laughing at?"

And the turtle said, "Why I see that you are turned horse, and that you have a small bird riding you, but the small bird is the better bird."

And the eagle said to her, "Go you about your business. This is a family affair between my brother, the lark, and myself."

THE LOVE SONG

A poet once wrote a love song and it was beautiful. And he made many copies of it, and sent them to his friends and his acquaintances, both men and women, and even to a young woman whom he had met but once, who lived beyond the mountains.

And in a day or two a messenger came from the young woman bringing a letter. And in the letter she said, "Let me assure you, I am deeply touched by the love song that you have written to me. Come now, and see my father and my mother, and we shall make arrangements for the betrothal."

And the poet answered the letter, and he said to her, "My friend, it was but a song of love out of a poet's heart, sung by every man to every woman."

And she wrote again to him saying, "Hypocrite and liar in words! From this day unto my coffin-day I shall hate all poets for your sake."

TEARS AND LAUGHTER

Upon the bank of the Nile at eventide, a hyena met a crocodile and they stopped and greeted one another.

The hyena spoke and said, "How goes the day with you, Sir?"

And the crocodile answered saying, "It goes badly with me. Sometimes in my pain and sorrow I weep, and then the creatures always say, 'They are but crocodile tears.' And this wounds me beyond all telling."

Then the hyena said, "You speak of your pain and your sorrow, but think of me also, for a moment. I gaze at the beauty of the world, its wonders and its miracles, and out of sheer joy I laugh even as the day laughs. And then the people of the jungle say, 'It is but the laughter of a hyena.'"

AT THE FAIR

There came to the Fair a girl from the country-side, most comely. There was a lily and a rose in her face. There was a sunset in her hair, and dawn smiled upon her lips.

No sooner did the lovely stranger appear in their sight than the young men sought her and surrounded her. One would dance with her, and another would cut a cake in her honour. And they all desired to kiss her cheek. For after all, was it not the Fair?

But the girl was shocked and started, and she thought ill of the young men. She rebuked them, and she even struck one or two of them in the face. Then she ran away from them.

And on her way home that evening she was saying in her heart, "I am disgusted. How unmannerly and ill bred are these men. It is beyond all patience."

A year passed during which that very comely girl thought much of Fairs and men. Then she came again to the Fair with the lily and the rose in her face, the sunset in her hair and the smile of dawn upon her lips.

But now the young men, seeing her, turned from her. And all the day long she was unsought and alone.

And at eventide as she walked the road toward her home she cried in her heart, "I am disgusted. How unmannerly and ill bred are these youths. It is beyond all patience."

THE TWO PRINCESSES

In the city of Shawakis lived a prince, and he was loved by everyone, men and women and children. Even the animals of the field came unto him in greeting.

But all the people said that his wife, the princess, loved him not; nay, that she even hated him.

And upon a day the princess of a neighbouring city came to visit the princess of Shawakis. And they sat and talked together, and their words led to their husbands.

And the princess of Sharakis said with passion, "I envy you your happiness with the prince, your husband, though you have been married these many years. I hate my husband. He belongs not to me alone, and I am indeed a woman most unhappy."

Then the visiting princess gazed at her and said, "My friend, the truth is that you love your husband. Aye, and you still have him for a passion unspent, and that is life in woman like unto Spring in a garden. But pity me, and my husband, for we do but endure one another in silent patience. And yet you and others deem this happiness."

THE LIGHTNING FLASH

There was a Christian bishop in his cathedral on a stormy day, and an un-Christian woman came and stood before him, and she said, "I am not a Christian. Is there salvation for me from hell-fire?"

And the bishop looked upon the woman, and he answered her saying, "Nay, there is salvation for those only who are baptized of water and of the spirit."

And even as he spoke a bolt from the sky fell with thunder upon the cathedral and it was filled with fire. And the men of the city came running, and they saved the woman, but the bishop was consumed, food of the fire.

THE HERMIT AND THE BEASTS

Once there lived among the green hills a hermit. He was pure of spirit and white of heart. And all the animals of the land and all the fowls of the air came to him in pairs and he spoke unto them. They heard him gladly, and they would gather near unto him, and would not go until nightfall, when he would send them away, entrusting them to the wind and the woods with his blessing.

Upon an evening as he was speaking of love, a leopard raised her head and said to the hermit, "You speak to us of loving. Tell us, Sir, where is your mate?"

And the hermit said, "I have no mate."

Then a great cry of surprise rose from the company of beasts and fowls, and they began to say among themselves, "How can he tell us of loving and mating when he himself knows naught thereof?" And quietly and in distain they left him alone.

That night the hermit lay upon his mat with his face earthward, and he wept bitterly and beat his hands upon his breast.

THE PROPHET AND THE CHILD

Once on a day the prophet Sharia met a child in a garden. The child ran to him and said, "Good morrow to you, Sir," and the prophet said, "Good morrow to you, Sir." And in a moment, "I see that you are alone."

Then the child said, in laughter and delight, "It took a long time to lose my nurse. She thinks I am behind those hedges; but can't you see that I am here?" Then he gazed at the prophet's face and spoke again. "You are alone, too. What did you do with your nurse?"

The prophet answered and said, "Ah, that is a different thing. In very truth I cannot lose her oftentime. But now, when I came into this garden, she was seeking after me behind the hedges."

The child clapped his hands and cried out, "So you are like me! Isn't it good to be lost?" And then he said, "Who are you?"

And the man answered, "They call me the prophet Sharia. And tell me, who are you?"

"I am only myself," said the child, "and my nurse is seeking after me, and she does not know where I am."

Then the prophet gazed into space saying, "I too have escaped my nurse for awhile, but she will find me out."

And the child said, "I know mine will find me out too."

At that moment a woman's voice was heard calling the child's name, "See," said the child, "I told you she would be finding me."

And at the same moment another voice was heard, "Where art thou, Sharia?"

And the prophet said, "See my child, they have found me also."

And turning his face upward, Sharia answered, "Here I am."

THE PEARL

Said one oyster to a neighbouring oyster, "I have a very great pain within me. It is heavy and round and I am in distress."

And the other oyster replied with haughty complacence, "Praise be to the heavens and to the sea, I have no pain within me. I am well and whole both within and without."

At that moment a crab was passing by and heard the two oysters, and he said to the one who was well and whole both within and without, "Yes, you are well and whole; but the pain that your neighbour bears is a pearl of exceeding beauty."

BODY AND SOUL

A man and a woman sat by a window that opened upon Spring. They sat close one unto the other. And the woman said, "I love you. You are handsome, and you are rich, and you are always well-attired."

And the man said, "I love you. You are a beautiful thought, a thing too apart to hold in the hand, and a song in my dreaming."

But the woman turned from him in anger, and she said, "Sir, please leave me now. I am not a thought, and I am not a thing that passes in your dreams. I am a woman. I would have you desire me, a wife, and the mother of unborn children."

And they parted.

And the man was saying in his heart, "Behold another dream is even now turned into mist."

And the woman was saying, "Well, what of a man who turns me into a mist and a dream?"

THE KING

The people of the kingdom of Sadik surrounded the palace of their king shouting in rebellion against him. And he came down the steps of the palace carrying his crown in one hand and his sceptre in the other. The majesty of his appearance silenced the multitude, and he stood before them and said, "My friends, who are no longer my subjects, here I yield my crown and sceptre unto you. I would be one of you. I am only one man, but as a man I would work together with you that our lot may be made better. There is no need for king. Let us go therefore to the fields and the vineyards and labour hand with hand. Only you must tell me to what field or vineyard I should go. All of you now are king."

And the people marvelled, and stillness was upon them, for the king whom they had deemed the source of their discontent now yielding his crown and sceptre to them and became as one of them.

Then each and every one of them went his way, and the king walked with one man to a field.

But the Kingdom of Sadik fared not better without a king, and the mist of discontent was still upon the land. The people cried out in the market places saying that they have a king to rule them. And the elders and the youths said as if with one voice, "We will have our king."

And they sought the king and found him toiling in the field, and they brought him to his seat, and yielded unto his crown and his sceptre. And they said, "Now rule us, with might and with justice."

And he said, "I will indeed rule you with might, and may the gods of the heaven and the earth help me that I may also rule with justice."

Now, there came to his presence men and women and spoke unto him of a baron who mistreated them, and to whom they were but serfs.

And straightway the king brought the baron before him and said, "The life of one man is as weighty in the scales of God as the life of another. And because you know not how to weigh the lives of those who work in your fiends and your vineyards, you are banished, and you shall leave this kingdom forever."

The following day came another company to the king and spoke of the cruelty of a countess beyond the hills, and how she brought them down to misery. Instantly the countess was brought to court, and the king sentenced her also to banishment, saying, "Those who till our fields and care for our vineyards are nobler than we who eat the bread they prepare and drink the wine of their wine-press. And because you know not this, you shall leave this land and be afar from this kingdom."

Then came men and women who said that the bishop made them bring stones and hew the stones for the cathedral, yet he gave them naught, though they knew the bishop's coffer was full of gold and silver while they themselves were empty with hunger.

And the king called for the bishop, and when the bishop came the king spoke and said unto his, "That cross you wear upon your bosom should mean giving life unto life. But you have taken life from life and you have given none. Therefore you shall leave this kingdom never to return."

Thus each day for a full moon men and women came to the king to tell him of the burdens laid upon them. And each and every day a full moon some oppressor was exiled from the land.

And the people of Sadik were amazed, and there was cheer in their heart.

And upon a day the elders and the youths came and surrounded the tower of the king and called for him. And he came down holding his crown with one hand and his sceptre with the other.

And he spoke unto and said, "Now, what would you do of me? Behold, I yield back to you that which you desired me to hold."

But they cried. "Nay, nay, you are our rightful king. You have made clean the land of vipers, and you have brought the wolves to naught, and we welcome to sing our thanksgiving unto you. The crown is yours in majesty and the sceptre is yours in glory."

Then the king said, "Not I, not I. You yourselves are king. When you deemed me weak and a misruler, you yourselves were weak and misruling. And now the land fares well because it is in your will. I am but a thought in the mind of you all, and I exist not save in your actions. There is no such person as governor. Only the governed exist to govern themselves."

And the king re-entered his tower with his crown and his sceptre. And the elders and the youths went their various ways and they were content.

And each and every one thought of himself as king with a crown in one hand and a sceptre in the other.

UPON THE SAND

Said one man to another, "At the high tide of the sea, long ago, with the point of my staff I wrote a line upon the sand; and the people still pause to read it, and they are careful that naught shall erase it."

And the other man said, "And I to wrote a line upon the sand, but it was at low tide, and the waves of the vast sea washed it away. But tell me, what did you write?"

And the first man answered and said, "I wrote this: 'I am he who is.' But what did you write?"

And the other man said, "This I wrote: 'I am but a drop of this great ocean.'"

THE THREE GIFTS

Once in the city of Becharre there lived a gracious prince who was loved and honoured by all his subjects.

But there was one exceedingly poor man who was bitter against the prince, and who wagged continually a pestilent tongue in his dispraise.

The prince knew this, yet he was patient.

But at last he bethought him; and upon a wintry night there came to the door of the man a servant of the prince, bearing a sack of flour, a bag of soap and a cone of sugar.

And the servant said, "The prince sends you these gifts in token of remembrance."

The man was elated, for he thought the gifts were an homage from the prince. And in his pride we went to the bishop and told him what the prince had done, saying, "Can you not see how the prince desires my goodwill?"

But the bishop said, "Oh, how wise a prince, and how little you understand. He speaks in symbols. The flour is for your empty stomach; the soap is for your dirty hide; and the sugar is to sweeten your bitter tongue."

From that day forward the man became shy even of himself. His hatred of the prince was greater than ever, and even more he hated the bishop who had revealed the prince unto him.

But thereafter he kept silent.

PEACE AND WAR

Three dogs were basking in the sun and conversing. The first dog said dreamily, "It is indeed wondrous to be living in this day of dogdom. Consider the ease with which we travel under the sea, upon the earth and even in the sky. And meditate for a moment upon the inventions brought forth for the comfort of dogs, even for our eyes and ears and noses."

And the second dog spoke and he said, "We are more heedful of the arts. We bark at the moon more rhythmically than did our forefathers. And when we gaze at ourselves in the water we see that our features are clearer than the features of yesterday."

Then the third dog spoke and said, "But what interests me most and beguiles my mind is the tranquil understanding existing between dogdoms."

At that very moment they looked, and lo, the dog-catcher was approaching.

The three dogs sprang up and scampered down the street; and as they ran the third dog said, "For God's sake, run for your lives. Civilization is after us."

THE DANCER

Once there came to the court of the Prince of Birkasha a dancer with her musicians. And she was admitted to the court, and she danced before the prince to the music the lute and the flute and the zither.

She danced the dance of flames, and the dance of swords and spears; she danced the dance of stars and the dance of space. And then she danced the dance of flowers in the wind.

After this she stood before the throne of the prince and bowed her body before him. And the prince bade her to come nearer, and he said unto her, "Beautiful woman, daughter of grace and delight, whence comes your art? And how is it that you command all the elements in your rhythms and your rhymes?"

And the dancer bowed again before the prince, and she answered, "Mighty and gracious Majesty, I know not the answer to your questionings. Only this I know: The philosopher's soul dwells in his head, the poet's soul is in the heart; the singer's soul lingers about his throat, but the soul of the dancer abides in all her body."

THE TWO GUARDIAN ANGELS

On an evening two angels met at the city gate, and they greeted one another, and they conversed.

The one angel said, "What are you doing these days, and what work is given you?"

And the other answered, "It was been assigned me to be the guardian of a fallen man who lives down in the valley, a great sinner, most degraded. Let me assure you it is an important task, and I work hard."

The first fallen angel said, "That is an easy commission. I have often known sinners, and have been their guardian many a time. But it has now been assigned me to be the guardian of the good saint who lives in a bower out yonder. And I assure you that is an exceedingly difficult work, and most subtle."

Said the first angel, "This is but assumption. How can guarding a saint be harder than guarding a sinner?"

And the other answered, "What impertinence, to call me assumptious! I have stated but the truth. Methinks it is you who are assumptious!"

Then the angels wrangled and fought, first with words and then with fists and wings.

While they were fighting an archangel came by. And he stopped them, and said, "Why do you fight? And what is it all about? Know you not that it is most unbecoming for guardian angels to fight at the city gate? Tell me, what is your disagreement?"

Then both angels spoke at once, each claiming that the work given him was the harder, and that he deserved the greater recognition.

The archangel shook his head and bethought him.

Then he said, "My friends, I cannot say now which one of you has the greater claim upon honour and reward. But since the power is bestowed in me, therefore for peace' sake and for good guardianship, I give each of you the other's occupation, since each of you insists that the other's task is the easier one. Now go hence and be happy at your work."

The angels thus ordered went their ways. But each one looked backward with greater anger at the archangel. And in his heart each was saying, "Oh, these archangels! Every day they make life harder and still harder for us angels!"

But the archangel stood there, and once more he bethought him. And he said in his heart, "We have indeed, to be watchful and to keep guard over our guardian angels."

THE STATUE

Once there lived a man among the hills who possessed a statue wrought by an ancient master. It lay at his door face downward and he was not mindful of it.

One day there passed by his house a man from the city, a man of knowledge, and seeing the statue he inquired of the owner if he would sell it.

The owner laughed and said, "And pray who would want to buy that dull and dirty stone?"

The man from the city said, "I will give you this piece of silver for it."

And the other man was astonished and delighted.

The statue was removed to the city, upon the back of and elephant. And after many moons the man from the hills visited the city, and as he walked the streets he saw a crowd before a shop, and a man with a loud voice was crying, "Come ye in and behold the most beautiful, the most wonderful statue in all the world. Only two silver pieces to look upon this most marvellous work of a master."

Thereupon the man from the hills paid two silver pieces and entered the shop to see the statue that he himself had sold for one spice of silver.

THE EXCHANGE

Once upon a crossroad a poor Poet met a rich Stupid, and they conversed. And all that they said revealed but their discontent.

Then the Angel of the Road passed by, and he laid his hand upon the shoulder of the two men.

And behold, a miracle: The two men had now exchanged their possessions.

And they parted. But strange to relate, the Poet looked and found naught in his hand but dry moving sand; and the Stupid closed his eyes and felt naught but moving cloud in his heart.

LOVE AND HATE

A woman said unto a man, "I love you." And the man said, "It is in my heart to be worthy of your love."

Ant he woman said, "You love me not?"

And the man only gazed upon her and said nothing.

Then the woman cried aloud, "I hate you."

And the man said, "Then it is also in my heart to be worthy of your hate."

DREAMS

A man dreamed a dream, and when he awoke he went to his soothsayer and desired that his dream be made plain unto him.

And the soothsayer said to the man, "Come to me with the dreams that you behold in your wakefulness and I will tell you their meaning. But the dreams of your sleep belong neither to my wisdom nor to your imagination."

THE MADMAN

It was in the garden of a madhouse that I met a youth with a face pale and lovely and full of wonder. And I sat beside him upon the bench, and I said, "Why are you here?"

And he looked at me in astonishment, and he said, "It is an unseemly question, yet I will answer you. My father would make of me a reproduction of himself; so also would my uncle. My mother would have me the image of her seafaring husband as the perfect example for me to follow. My brother thinks I should be like him, a fine athlete.

"And my teachers also, the doctor of philosophy, and the music-master, and the logician, they too were determined, and each would have me but a reflection of his own face in a mirror.

"Therefore I came to this place. I find it more sane here. At least, I can be myself."

Then of a sudden he turned to me and he said, "But tell me, were you also driven to this place by education and good counsel?"

And I answered, "No, I am a visitor."

And he answered, "Oh, you are one of those who live in the madhouse on the other side of the wall."

THE FROGS

Upon a summer day a frog said to his mate, "I fear those people living in that house on the shore are disturbed by our night-songs."

And his mate answered and said, "Well, do they not annoy our silence during the day with their talking?"

The frog said, "Let us not forget that we may sing too much in the night."

And his mate answered, "Let us not forget that they chatter and shout overmuch during the day."

Said the frog, "How about the bullfrog who that they clatter and shout overmuch during the day."

Said the frog, "How about the bullfrog who disturbs the whole neighbourhood with his God-forbidden booming?"

And his mate replied, "Aye, and what say you of the politician and the priest and the scientist who come to these shores and fill the air with noisy and rhymeless sound?"

Then the frog said, "Well, let us be better than these human beings. Let us be quiet at night, and keep our songs in our hearts, even though the moon calls for our rhythm and the stars for our rhyme. At least, let us be silent for a night or two, or even for three nights."

And his mate said, "Very well, I agree. We shall see what your bountiful heart will bring forth."

That night the frogs were silent; and they were silent the following night also, and again upon the third night.

And strange to relate, the talkative woman who lived in the house beside the lake came down to breakfast on that third day and shouted to her husband, "I have not slept these three nights. I was secure with sleep when the noise of the frogs was in my ear. But something must have happened. They have not sung now for three nights; and I am almost maddened with sleeplessness."

The frog heard this and turned to his mate and said, winking his eye, "And we were almost maddened with our silence, were we not?"

And his mate answered, "Yes, the silence of the night was heavy upon us. And I can see now that there is no need for us to cease our singing for the comfort of those who must needs fill their emptiness with noise."

And that night the moon called not in vain for their rhythm nor the stars for their rhyme.

LAWS AND LAW-GIVING

Ages ago there was a great king, and he was wise. And he desired to lay laws unto his subjects.

He called upon one thousand wise men of one thousand different tribes to his capitol and lay down the laws.

And all this came to pass.

But when the thousand laws written upon parchment were put before the king and he read them, he wept bitterly in his soul, for he had not known that there were one thousand forms of crime in his kingdom.

Then he called his scribe, and with a smile upon his mouth he himself dictated laws. And his laws were but seven.

And the one thousand wise men left him in anger and returned to their tribes with the laws they had laid down. And every tribe followed the laws of its wise men.

Therefore they have a thousand laws even to our own day.

It is a great country, but it has one thousand prisons, and the prisons are full of women and men, breakers of a thousand laws.

It is indeed a great country, but the people thereof are descendants of one thousand law-givers and of only one wise king.

YESTERDAY, TODAY AND TOMORROW

I said to my friend, "You see her leaning upon the arm of that man. It was but yesterday that she leaned thus upon my arm."

And my friend said, "And tomorrow she will lean upon mine."

I said, "Behold her sitting close at his side. It was but yesterday she sat close beside me."

And he answered, "Tomorrow she will sit beside me."

I said, "See, she drinks wine from his cup, and yesterday she drank from mine."

And he said, "Tomorrow, from my cup."

Then I said, "See how she gazes at him with love, and with yielding eyes. Yesterday she gazed thus upon me."

And my friend said, "It will be upon me she gazes tomorrow."

I said, "Do you not hear her now murmuring songs of love into his ears? Those very songs of love she murmured but yesterday into my ears."

And my friend said, "And tomorrow she will murmur them in mine."

I said, "Why see, she is embracing him. It was but yesterday that she embraced me."

And my friend said, "She will embrace me tomorrow."

Then I said, "What a strange woman."

But he answered, "She is like unto life, possessed by all men; and like death, she conquers all men; and like eternity, she enfolds all men."

THE PHILOSOPHER AND THE COBBLER

There came to a cobbler's shop a philosopher with worn shoes. And the philosopher said to the cobbler, "Please mend my shoes."

And the cobbler said, "I am mending another man's shoes now, and there are still other shoes to patch before I can come to yours. But leave your shoes here, and wear this other pair today, and come tomorrow for your own."

Then the philosopher was indignant, and he said, "I wear no shoes that are not mine own."

And the cobbler said, "Well then, are you in truth a philosopher, and cannot enfold your feet with the shoes of another man? Upon this very street there is another cobbler who understands philosophers better than I do. Go you to him for mending."

BUILDERS OF BRIDGES

In Antioch where the river Assi goes to meet the sea, a bridge was built to bring one half of the city nearer to the other half. It was built of large stones carried down from among the hills, on the backs of the mules of Antioch.

When the bridge was finished, upon a pillar thereof was engraved in Greek and in Aramaic, "This bridge was builded by King Antiochus II."

And all the people walked across the good bridge over the goodly river Assi.

And upon an evening, a youth, deemed by some a little mad, descended to the pillar where the words were engraven, and he covered over the graving with charcoal, and above it wrote, "The stones of this bridge were brought down from the hills by the mules. In passing to and fro over it you are riding upon the backs of the mules of Antioch, builders of this bridge."

And when the people read what the youth had written, some of them laughed and some marvelled. And some said, "Ah yes, we know who has done this. Is he not a little mad?"

But one mule said, laughing, to another mule, "Do you not remember that we did carry those stones? And yet until now it has been said that the bridge was builded by King Antiochus."

THE FIELD OF ZAAD

Upon the road of Zaad a traveller met a man who lived in a nearby village, and the traveller, pointing with his hand to a vast field, asked the man saying, "Was not this the battle-ground where King Ahlam overcame his enemies?"

And the man answered and said, "This has never been a battle-ground. There once stood on this field the great city of Zaad, and it was burnt down to ashes. But now it is a good field, is it not?"

And the traveller and the man parted.

Not a half mile farther the traveller met another man, and pointing to the field again, he said, "So that is where the great city of Zaad once stood?'

And the man said, "There has never been a city in this place. But once there was a monastery here, and it was destroyed by the people of the South Country."

Shortly after, on that very road of Zaad, the traveller met a third man, and pointing once more to the vast field he said, "Is it not true that this is the place where once there stood a great monastery?"

But the man answered, "There has never been a monastery in this neighbourhood, but our fathers and our forefathers have told us that once there fell a great meteor on this field."

Then the traveller walked on, wondering in his heart. And he met a very old man, and saluting his he said, "Sir, upon this road I have met three men who live in the neighbourhood and I have asked each of them about this field, and each one denied what the other had said, and each one told me a new tale that the other had not told."

Then the old man raised his head, and answered, "My friend, each and every one of these men told you what was indeed so; but few of us are able to add fact to different fact and make a truth thereof."

THE GOLDEN BELT

Once upon a day two men who met on the road were walking together toward Salamis, the City of Columns. In the mid-afternoon they came to a wide river and there was no bridge to cross it. They must needs swim, or seek another road unknown to them.

And they said to one another, "Let us swim. After all, the river is not so wide." And they threw themselves into the water and swam.

And one of the men who had always known rivers and the ways of rivers, in mid-stream suddenly began to lose himself; and to be carried away by the rushing waters; while the other who had never swum before crossed the river straight-way and stood upon the farther bank. Then seeing his companion still wrestling with the stream, he threw himself again into the waters and brought him also safely to the shore.

And the man who had been swept away by the current said, "But you told me you could not swim. How then did you cross that river with such assurance?"

And the second man answered, "My friend, do you see this belt which girdles me? It is full of golden coins that I have earned for my wife and my children, a full year's work. It is the weight of this belt of gold that carried me across the river, to my wife and my children. And my wife and my children were upon my shoulders as I swam."

And the two men walked on together toward Salamis.

THE RED EARTH

Said a tree to a man, "My roots are in the deep red earth, and I shall give you of my fruit."

And the man said to the tree, "How alike we are. My roots are also deep in the red earth. And the red earth gives you power to bestow upon me of your fruit, and the red earth teaches me to receive from you with thanksgiving."

THE FULL MOON

The full moon rose in glory upon the town, and all the dogs of that town began to bark at the moon.

Only one dog did not bark, and he said to them in a grave voice, "Awake not stillness from her sleep, nor bring you the moon to the earth with your barking."

Then all the dogs ceased barking, in awful silence. But the dog who had spoken to them continued barking for silence, the rest of the night.

THE HERMIT PROPHET

Once there lived a hermit prophet, and thrice a moon he would go down to the great city and in the market places he would preach giving and sharing to the people. And he was eloquent, and his fame was upon the land.

Upon an evening three men came to his hermitage and he greeted them. And they said, "You have been preaching giving and sharing, and you have sought to teach those who have much to give unto those who have little; and we doubt not that your fame has brought you riches. Now come and give us of your riches, for we are in need."

And the hermit answered and said, "My friends, I have naught but this bed and this mat and this jug of water. Take them if it is in your desire. I have neither gold nor silver."

Then they looked down with distain upon him, and turned their faces from him, and the last man stood at the door for a moment, and said, "Oh, you cheat! You fraud! You teach and preach that which you yourself do not perform."

THE OLD, OLD WINE

Once there lived a rich man who was justly proud of his cellar and the wine therein. And there was one jug of ancient vintage kept for some occasion known only to himself.

The governor of the state visited him, and he bethought him and said, "That jug shall not be opened for a mere governor."

And a bishop of the diocese visited him, but he said to himself, "Nay, I will not open that jug. He would not know its value, nor would its aroma reach his nostrils."

The prince of the realm came and supped with him. But he thought, "It is too royal a wine for a mere princeling."

And even on the day when his own nephew was married, he said to himself, "No, not to these guests shall that jug be brought forth."

And the years passed by, and he died, an old man, and he was buried like unto every seed and acorn.

And upon the day that he was buried the ancient jug was brought out together with other jugs of wine, and it was shared by the peasants of the neighbourhood. And none knew its great age.

To them, all that is poured into a cup is only wine.

THE TWO POEMS

Many centuries ago, on a road to Athens, two poets met, and they were glad to see one another.

And one poet asked the other saying, "What have you composed of late, and how goes it with your lyre?"

And the other poet answered and said with pride, "I have but now finished the greatest of my poems, perchance the greatest poem yet written in Greek. It is an invocation to Zeus the Supreme."

Then he took from beneath his cloak a parchment, saying, "Here, behold, I have it with me, and I would fain read it to you. Come, let us sit in the shade of that white cypress."

And the poet read his poem. And it was a long poem.

And the other poet said in kindliness, "This is a great poem. It will live through the ages, and in it you shall be glorified."

And the first poet said calmly, "And what have you been writing these late days?"

And the other another, "I have written but little. Only eight lines in remembrance of a child playing in a garden." And he recited the lines.

The first poet said, "Not so bad; not so bad."

And they parted.

And now after two thousand years the eight lines of the one poet are read in every tongue, and are loved and cherished.

And though the other poem has indeed come down through the ages in libraries and in the cells of scholars, and though it is remembered, it is neither loved nor read.

LADY RUTH

Three men once looked from afar upon a white house that stood alone on a green hill. One of them said, "That is the house of Lady Ruth. She is an old witch."

The second man said, "You are wrong. Lady Ruth is a beautiful woman who lives there consecrated unto her dreams."

The third man said, "You are both wrong. Lady Ruth is the holder of this vast land, and she draws blood from her serfs."

And they walked on discussing Lady Ruth. Then when they came to a crossroad they met an old man, and one of them asked him, saying, "Would you please tell us about the Lady Ruth who lives in that white house upon the hill?"

And the old man raised his head and smiled upon them, and said, "I am ninety of years, and I remember Lady Ruth when I was but a boy. But Lady Ruth died eighty years ago, and now the house is empty. The owls hoot therein, sometimes, and people say the place is haunted."

THE MOUSE AND THE CAT

Once on an evening a poet met a peasant. The poet was distant and the peasant was shy, yet they conversed.

And the peasant said, "Let me tell you a little story which I heard of late. A mouse was caught in a trap, and while he was happily eating the cheese that lay therein, a cat stood by. The mouse trembled awhile, but he knew he was safe within the trap.

"Then the cat said, 'You are eating your last meal, my friend.'

"'Yes,' answered the mouse, 'one life have I, therefore one death. But what of you? They tell me you have nine lives. Doesn't that mean that you will have to die nine times?'"

And the peasant looked at the poet and he said, "Is not this a strange story?"

And the poet answered him not, but he walked away saying in his soul, "To be sure, nine lives have we, nine lives to be sure. And we shall die nine times, nine times shall we die. Perhaps it were better to have but one life, caught in a trap—the life of a peasant with a bit of cheese for the last meal. And yet, are we not kin unto the lions of the desert and the jungle?"

THE CURSE

And old man of the sea once said to me, "It was thirty years ago that a sailor ran away with my daughter. And I cursed them both in my heart, for of all the world I loved but my daughter.

"Not long after that, the sailor youth went down with his ship to the bottom of the sea, and with him my lovely daughter was lost unto me.

"Now therefore behold in me the murderer of a youth and a maid. It was my curse that destroyed them. And now on my way to the grave I seek God's forgiveness."

This the old man said. But there was a tone of bragging in his words, and it seems that he is still proud of the power of his curse.

THE POMEGRANATES

There was once a man who had many pomegranate trees in his orchard. And for many an autumn he would put his pomegranates on silvery trays outside of his dwelling, and upon the trays he would place signs upon which he himself had written, "Take one for aught. You are welcome."

But people passed by and no one took of the fruit.

Then the man bethought him, and one autumn he placed no pomegranates on silvery trays outside of his dwelling, but he raised this sign in large lettering: "Here we have the best pomegranates in the land, but we sell them for more silver than any other pomegranates."

And now behold, all the men and women of the neighbourhood came rushing to buy.

GOD AND MANY GODS

In the city of Kilafis a sophist stood on the steps of the Temple and preached many gods. And the people said in their hearts, "We know all this. Do they not live with us and follow us wherever we go?"

Not long after, another man stood in the market place and spoke unto the people and said, "There is no god." And many who heard him were glad of his tidings, for they were afraid of gods.

And upon another day there came a man of great eloquence, an he said, "There is but one God." And now the people were dismayed for in their hearts they feared the judgment of one God more than that of many gods.

That same season there came yet another man, and he said to the people, "There are three gods, and they dwell upon the wind as one, and they have a vast and gracious mother who is also their mate and their sister."

Then everyone was comforted, for they said in their secret, "three gods in one must needs disagree over our failings, and besides, their gracious mother will surely be an advocate for us poor weaklings."

Yet even to this day there are those in the city of Kilafis who wrangle and argue with each other about many gods and no god, and one god and three gods in one, and a gracious mother of gods.

SHE WHO WAS DEAF

Once there lived a rich man who had a young wife, and she was stone deaf.

And upon a morning when they were breaking their feast, she spoke to him and she said, "Yesterday I visited the market place, and there were exhibited silken raiment from Damascus, and coverchiefs from India, necklaces from Persia, and bracelets from Yamman. It seems that the caravans had but just brought these things to our city. And now behold me, in rags, yet the wife of a rich man. I would have some of those beautiful things."

The husband, still busy with his morning coffee said, "My dear, there is no reason why you should not go down to the Street and buy all that your heart may desire."

And the deaf wife said, "'No!' You always say, 'No, no.' Must I needs appear in tatters among our friends to shame your wealth and my people?"

And the husband said, "I did not say, 'No.' You may go forth freely to the market place and purchase the most beautiful apparel and jewels that have come to our city."

But again the wife mis-read his words, and she replied, "Of all rich men you are the most miserly. You would deny me everything of beauty and loveliness, while other women of my age walk the gardens of the city clothed in rich raiment."

And she began to weep. And as her tears fell upon her breast she cried out again, "You always say, 'Nay, nay' to me when I desire a garment or a jewel."

Then the husband was moved, and he stood up and took out of his purse a handful of gold and placed it before her, saying in a kindly voice, "Go down to the market place, my dear, and buy all that you will."

From that day onward the deaf young wife, whenever she desired anything, would appear before her husband with a pearly tear in her eye, and he in silence would take out a handful of gold and place it in her lap.

Now, it changed that the young woman fell in love with a youth whose habit it was to make long journeys. And whenever he was away she would sit in her casement and weep.

When her husband found her thus weeping, he would say in his heart, "There must be some new caravan, and some silken garments and rare jewels in the Street."

And he would take a handful of gold and place it before her.

THE QUEST

A thousand years ago two philosophers met on a slope of Lebanon, and one said to the other, "Where goest thou?"

And the other answered, "I am seeking after the fountain of youth which I know wells out among these hills. I have found writings which tell of that fountain flowering toward the sun. And you, what are you seeking?"

The first man answered, "I am seeking after the mystery of death."

Then each of the two philosophers conceived that the other was lacking in his great science, and they began to wrangle, and to accuse each other of spiritual blindness.

Now while the two philosophers were loud upon the wind, a stranger, a man who was deemed a simpleton in his own village, passed by, and when he heard the two in hot dispute, he stood awhile and listened to their argument.

Then he came near to them and said, "My good men, it seems that you both really belong to the same school of philosophy, and that you are speaking of the same thing, only you speak in different words. One of you is seeks the fountain of youth, and the other seeks the mystery of death. Yet indeed they are but one, and as they dwell in you both."

Then the stranger turned away saying, "Farewell sages." And as he departed he laughed a patient laughter.

The two philosophers looked at each other in silence for a moment, and then they laughed also. And one of them said, "Well now, shall we not walk and seek together."

THE SCEPTRE

Said a king to his wife, "Madame, you are not truly a queen. You are too vulgar and ungracious to be my mate."

Said his wife, "Sir, you deem yourself king, but indeed you are only a poor soundling."

Now these words angered the king, and he took his sceptre with his hand, and struck the queen upon her forehead with his golden sceptre.

At that moment the lord chamberlain entered, and he said, "Well, well, Majesty! That sceptre was fashioned by the greatest artist of the land. Alas! Some day you and the queen shall be forgotten, but this sceptre shall be kept, a thing of beauty from generation to generation. And now that you have drawn blood from her Majesty's head, Sire, the sceptre shall be the more considered and remembered."

THE PATH

There lived among the hills a woman and her son, and he was her first-born and her only child.

And the boy died of a fever whilst the physician stood by.

The mother was distraught with sorrow, and she cried to the physician and besought him saying, "Tell me, tell me, what was it that made quiet his striving and silent his song?"

And the physician said, "It was the fever."

And the mother said, "What is the fever?"

And the physician answered, "I cannot explain it. It is a thing infinitely small that visits the body, and we cannot see it with the human eye."

The physician left her. And she kept repeating to herself, "Something infinitely small. We cannot see it with our human eye."

And at evening the priest came to console her. And she wept and she cried out saying, "Oh, why have I lost my son, my only son, my first-born?"

And the priest answered, "My child, it is the will of God."

And the woman said, "What is God and where is God? I would see God that I may tear my bosom before Him, and pour the blood of my heart at His feet. Tell me where I shall find Him."

And the priest said, ""God is infinitely vast. He is not to be seen with our human eye."

Then the woman cried out, "The infinitely small has slain my son through the will of the infinitely great! Then what are we? What are we?"

At that moment the woman's mother came into the room with the shroud for the dead boy, and she heard the words of the priest and also her daughter's cry. And she laid down the shroud, and took her daughter's hand in her own hand, and she said, "My daughter, we ourselves are the infinitely small and the infinitely great; and we are the path between the two."

THE WHALE AND THE BUTTERFLY

Once on an evening a man and a woman found themselves together in a stagecoach. They had met before.

The man was a poet, and as he sat beside the woman he sought to amuse her with stories, some that were of his own weaving, and some that were not his own.

But even while he was speaking the lady went to sleep. Then suddenly the coach lurched, and she awoke, and she said, "I admire your interpretation of the story of Jonah and the whale."

And the poet said, "But Madame, I have been telling you a story of mine own about a butterfly and a white rose, and how they behaved the one to the other!"

THE SHADOW

Upon a June day the grass said to the shadow of an elm tree, "You move to right and left over-often, and you disturb my peace."

And the shadow answered and said, "Not I, not I. Look skyward. There is a tree that moves in the wind to the east and to the west, between the sun and the earth."

And the grass looked up, and for the first time beheld the tree. And it said in its heart, "Why, behold, there is a larger grass than myself."

And the grass was silent.

PEACE CONTAGIOUS

One branch in bloom said to his neighbouring branch, "This is a dull and empty day." And the other branch answered, "It is indeed empty and dull."

At that moment a sparrow alighted on one of the branches, and the another sparrow, nearby.

And one of the sparrows chirped and said, "My mate has left me."

And the other sparrow cried, "My mate has also gone, and she will not return. And what care I?"

Then the two birds began to twitter and scold, and soon they were fighting and making harsh noise upon the air.

All of a sudden two other sparrows came sailing from the sky, and they sat quietly beside the restless two. And there was calm, and there was peace.

Then the four flew away together in pairs.

And the first branch said to his neighbouring branch, "That was a mighty zig-zag of sound."

And the other branch answered, "Call it what you will, it is now both peaceful and spacious. And if the upper air makes peace it seems to me that those who dwell in the lower might make peace also. Will you not wave in the wind a little nearer to me?"

And the first branch said, "Oh, perchance, for peace' sake, ere the Spring is over."

And then he waved himself with the strong wind to embrace her.

SEVENTY

The poet youth said to the princess, "I love you." And the princess answered, "And I love you too, my child."

"But I am not your child. I am a man and I love you."

And she said, "I am the mother of sons and daughters, and they are fathers and mothers of sons and daughters; and one of the sons of my sons is older than you."

And the poet youth said, "But I love you."

It was not long after that the princess died. But ere her last breath was received again by the greater breath of earth, she said within her soul, "My beloved, mine only son, my youth-poet, it may yet be that some day we shall meet again, and I shall not be seventy."

FINDING GOD

Two men were walking in the valley, and one man pointed with his finger toward the mountain side, and said, "See you that hermitage? There lives a man who has long divorced the world. He seeks but after God, and naught else upon this earth."

And the other man said, "He shall not find God until he leaves his hermitage, and the aloneness of his hermitage, and returns to our world, to share our joy and pain, to dance with our dancers at the wedding feast, and to weep with those who weep around the coffins of our dead."

And the other man was convinced in his heart, though in spite of his conviction he answered, "I agree with all that you say, yet I believe the hermit is a good man. And it may it not well be that one good man by his absence does better than the seeming goodness of these many men?"

THE RIVER

In the valley of Kadisha where the mighty river flows, two little streams met and spoke to one another.

One stream said, "How came you, my friend, and how was your path?"

And the other answered, "My path was most encumbered. The wheel of the mill was broken, and the master farmer who used to conduct me from my channel to his plants, is dead. I struggled down oozing with the filth of laziness in the sun. But how was your path, my brother?"

And the other stream answered and said, "Mine was a different path. I came down the hills among fragrant flowers and shy willows; men and women drank of me with silvery cups, and little children paddled their rosy feet at my edges, and there was laughter all about me, and there were sweet songs. What a pity that your path was not so happy."

At that moment the river spoke with a loud voice and said, "Come in, come in, we are going to the sea. Come in, come in, speak no more. Be with me now. We are going to the sea. Come in, come in, for in me you shall forget you wanderings, sad or gay. Come in, come in. And you and I will forget all our ways when we reach the heart of our mother the sea."

THE TWO HUNTERS

Upon a day in May, Joy and Sorrow met beside a lake. They greeted one another, and they sat down near the quiet waters and conversed.

Joy spoke of the beauty which is upon the earth, and the daily wonder of life in the forest and among the hills, and of the songs heard at dawn and eventide.

And sorrow spoke, and agreed with all that Joy had said; for Sorrow knew the magic of the hour and the beauty thereof. And Sorrow was eloquent when he spoke of may in the fields and among the hills.

And Joy and Sorrow talked long together, and they agreed upon all things of which they knew.

Now there passed by on the other side of the lake two hunters. And as they looked across the water one of them said, "I wonder who are those two persons?" And the other said, "Did you say two? I see only one."

The first hunter said, "But there are two." And the second said, "There is only one that I can see, and the reflection in the lake is only one."

"Nay, there are two," said the first hunter, "and the reflection in the still water is of two persons."

But the second man said again, "Only one do I see." And again the other said, "But I see two so plainly."

And even unto this day one hunter says that the other sees double; while the other says, "My friend is somewhat blind."

THE OTHER WANDERER

Once on a time I met another man of the roads. He too was a little mad, and thus spoke to me:

"I am a wanderer. Oftentimes it seems that I walk the earth among pygmies. And because my head is seventy cubits farther from the earth than theirs, it creates higher and freer thoughts.

"But in truth I walk not among men but above them, and all they can see of me is my footprints in their open fields.

"And often have I heard them discuss and disagree over the shape and size of my footprints. For there are some who say, 'These are the tracks of a mammoth that roamed the earth in the far past.' And others say, 'Nay, these are places where meteors have fallen from the distant stars.'

"But you, my friend, you know full well that they are naught save the footprints of a wanderer."

Lightning Source UK Ltd.
Milton Keynes UK
15 October 2009

145014UK00001B/191/P

9 781406 829143